GOD'S MASTERWORK

A Concerto in Sixty-Six Movements

Volume Two

Ezra through Daniel

From the Bible-teaching ministry of

CHARLES R. SWINDOLL

INSIGHT FOR LIVING

Chuck graduated in 1963 from Dallas Theological Seminary, where he now serves as the school's fourth president, helping to prepare a new generation of men and women for the ministry. Chuck has served in pastorates in three states: Massachusetts, Texas, and California, including almost twenty-three years at the First Evangelical Free Church in Fullerton, California. His sermon messages have been aired over radio since 1979 as the *Insight for Living* broadcast. A best-selling author, Chuck has written numerous books and booklets on many subjects.

Based on the outlines and transcripts of Chuck's sermons, the study guide text is co-authored by Gary Matlack, a graduate of Texas Tech University and Dallas Theological Seminary. He also wrote the Living Insights sections.

Editor in Chief:
Cynthia Swindoll

Coauthor of Text:
Gary Matlack

Assistant Editor and Writer:
Wendy Peterson

Copy Editors:
Tom Kimber
Marco Salazar

Cover Designer:
Nina Paris

Text Designer:
Gary Lett

Graphics System Administrator:
Bob Haskins

Publishing System Specialist:
Alex Pasieka

Director, Communications Division:
John Norton

Marketing Manager:
Alene Cooper

Project Coordinator:
Colette Muse

Printer:
Sinclair Printing Company

Unless otherwise identified, all Scripture references are from the New American Standard Bible, © The Lockman Foundation 1960, 1962, 1963, 1968, 1971, 1972, 1973, 1975, 1977. Used by permission. Scripture taken from the Holy Bible, New International Version © 1973, 1978, 1984 International Bible Society, used by permission of Zondervan Bible Publishers.

Guide coauthored by Gary Matlack:
Copyright © 1997 by Charles R. Swindoll, Inc.

Original outlines, charts, and transcripts:
Copyright © 1979, 1980 by Charles R. Swindoll.

Unless otherwise indicated, all charts are adapted from *The Living Insights Study Bible*, copyright © 1996 by the Zondervan Corporation.

An effort has been made to locate sources and obtain permission where necessary for the quotations used in this book. In the event of any unintentional omission, a modification will gladly be incorporated in future printings.

Series ISBN 0-8499-1474-4—*God's Masterwork: A Concerto in Sixty-Six Movements*
Study guide ISBN 0-8499-8739-3—*Volume Two: Ezra–Daniel*
COVER PHOTOGRAPHY: Richard Glenn
COVER BACKGROUND PHOTO: Superstock
Printed in the United States of America

CONTENTS

1 Ezra: True Man of the Word 1
   A Survey of Ezra

2 Nehemiah: Softhearted Hard Hat 12
   A Survey of Nehemiah

3 Esther: Beauty and the Best 22
   A Survey of Esther

4 Job: Magnificent Man of Misery 31
   A Survey of Job

5 Psalms: Inspired Anthology of Praise. 41
   A Survey of Psalms

6 Proverbs: Reliable Counsel for Right Living. 50
   A Survey of Proverbs

7 Ecclesiastes: Searching for the Meaning of Life 59
   A Survey of Ecclesiastes

8 Song of Solomon: Poem of Faithful Love 67
   A Survey of Song of Solomon

9 Profile of a Prophet 77
   Selected Scriptures

10 Isaiah: Prince among the Prophets. 86
   A Survey of Isaiah

11 Jeremiah: Weeping, Warning, and Waiting 97
   A Survey of Jeremiah

12 Lamentations: A Prophet's Broken Heart 107
   A Survey of Lamentations

13 Ezekiel: Strong Man of God 117
   A Survey of Ezekiel

14 Daniel: Man of Integrity, Message of Prophecy 128
   A Survey of Daniel

Books for Probing Further. 137

Ordering Information/Order Forms. 139

INTRODUCTION

One of the things that has always attracted me to the Bible is its intense practicality. Even the prophetic passages and the great doctrinal discourses were designed to get into our lives and change us.

That's why I'm excited about sharing volume 2 of *God's Masterwork* with you. From the down-in-the-trenches leadership of Ezra and Nehemiah, through the emotion-rich strains of the Psalms, to the unbending integrity of Daniel, the connectedness of God's Word to real life is undeniable.

I hope you will be as thrilled as I am to trace the sweep of history, the undercurrents of doctrine, and the pulse of redemption through this section of Scripture. And along the way, as is always the case with God's Word, you'll have plenty of opportunies for personal growth.

May God meet you, instruct you, challenge you, and change you as you continue to study His masterwork.

Chuck Swindoll

Chuck Swindoll

PUTTING TRUTH
INTO ACTION

Knowledge apart from application falls short of God's desire for His children. He wants us to apply what we learn so that we will change and grow. This study guide was prepared with these goals in mind. As you go through the following pages, we hope your desire to discover biblical truth will grow as your understanding of God's Word increases and that you will be encouraged to apply what you've learned.

To assist you in your study, we've included a section called **Living Insights** at the end of each lesson. These exercises will challenge you to study further and to think of specific ways to put your discoveries into action.

There are many ways to use this guide—in personal devotions, group studies, discussions with friends and family, and Sunday school classes. And, of course, it's an ideal study aid when you're listening to its corresponding *Insight for Living* radio series.

To benefit most from this study guide, we would encourage you to consider it a spiritual journal. That's why we've included space in the **Living Insights** for recording your thoughts and discoveries. We hope you'll return to those sections often for review and encouragement as you continue to grow in your walk with Christ.

Gary Matlack

Gary Matlack
Coauthor of Text
Author of Living Insights

GOD'S *MASTERWORK*

A Concerto in Sixty-Six Movements

Volume Two

Ezra through Daniel

Chapter 1

EZRA: TRUE MAN
OF THE WORD

A Survey of Ezra

Since the Fall of Adam and Eve in Genesis 3, the steady flow of
God's redemptive purposes has continued against the backdrop
of personal and national turmoil.

Genesis through 2 Chronicles trace the ups and downs of Israel,
which was meant to be a holy nation but didn't live up to God's
expectation for them. Because of their unfaithfulness, idolatry, and
immorality, the northern tribes were dismantled by Assyria, and the
southern tribes endured seventy years of Babylonian captivity. But
though they were chastised by God, they would always be His
chosen people.

The ray of hope at the end of 2 Chronicles fans into full sunlight
in the book of Ezra, as the exiles return home to Jerusalem. Ezra's
message reminds us that God's discipline, though often severe, has
as its goal our repentance and restoration. The same sovereign hand
that disciplines us holds onto us and eventually brings us back where
we belong—to Him.

Historical Context

By the time we get to the book of Ezra, the Promised Land is
a plundered land. Jerusalem was destroyed in Babylon's third and
final assault on Judah (586 B.C.), and the temple lay in charred
ruins. But as Ezra shows us, nothing, not even captivity, can thwart
God's preservation and restoration of His people.

1

EZRA

CENSUS AND JOURNEY — CHAPTERS 1–2

Construction
Leader: Zerubbabel

Temple
- Foundation
- Opposition
- Determination
- Completion

CHAPTERS 3–6

CENSUS AND JOURNEY — CHAPTERS 7–8

Reformation
Leader: Ezra

Revival
- Condition
- Confession
- Covenant
- Cleansing

CHAPTERS 9–10

CHRONICLES | ESTHER | NEHEMIAH

Emphasis	Construction of the temple			Reformation of the people	
Persian King	Cyrus	Darius	Xerxes	Artaxerxes	
Scope	National	General	Personal	Specific	
Theme	Revival and Reformation				
Key Verses	1:1–4; 3:2; 7:10				
Christ in Ezra	His birth anticipated in the preservation of the Davidic line and the remnant's return to the Promised Land. His work as spiritual rebuilder and restorer pictured in Zerubbabel and Ezra. His mediating presence and glory pictured in the altar and the temple.				

2

The Fall of Babylon, the Rise of Persia

In a divine twist of irony, God raised up a nation to overthrow the nation that had overthrown His people. The Babylonians, who had served as instruments of God's discipline, fell to Cyrus of Persia in October 539 B.C.

In Cyrus' first year as king, God moved the monarch's heart to issue a decree allowing the Jews to return to their homeland and rebuild the temple (see 2 Chron. 36:22–23; Ezra 4:1–4; see also Isa. 44:24–28). Just as God had used a pagan king, Nebuchadnezzar, to discipline His people, He raised up another pagan king, Cyrus—and later, Artaxerxes—to deliver them. In stirring these men to act kindly toward the Jews, God proved once again that the hearts of kings and the power of kingdoms are at His disposal to fashion His good and perfect will (see Prov. 21:1).

Chronology of Persian Kings Related to the Old Testament			
King	Dates (all B.C.)	Chapters in Ezra	Other Books
Cyrus	538–530	1:1–4:5	
Cambyses	530–522		
Smerdis	522		
Darius I	521–486	chaps. 5–6	Haggai (520), Zechariah (520–515)
Xerxes I (Ahasuerus)	486–465	4:6	Esther (474)
Artaxerxes I	464–423	4:7–23; chaps. 7–10	Malachi (450–400), Nehemiah (445–425)
Darius II			

The Second Exodus

The Jews' return from Babylon to Jerusalem has been called the "second exodus." Unlike the first, when all the Israelites streamed out of Egypt, only a remnant wanted to go home this time.

> Out of a total Jewish population of perhaps two or three million, only 49,897 choose to take advantage of this offer. Only the most committed are willing

to leave a life of relative comfort in Babylonia, endure a trek of nine hundred miles, and face further hardship by rebuilding a destroyed temple and city.[1]

Those Jews who took up the challenge of following God back to their homeland returned in three waves—just as they had been exiled in three deportations (605, 597, and 586 B.C.). The first return, shortly after Cyrus' decree in 538 B.C., brought the 49,897 mentioned above home to rebuild the temple under Zerubbabel's leadership. The second wave of returnees, only 1,754 people, set out eighty years later, in 458 B.C. In this second group was Ezra, who arrived in Jerusalem with a passion to preach the Scriptures and call the community to holy living. Fourteen years later, in 444 B.C., a third group returned under Nehemiah to rebuild the wall around Jerusalem.

The book of Ezra covers the first two returns. Sandwiched between the first and second returns is an eighty-year period in which the events recorded in Esther took place. The third return is recorded in the book of Nehemiah.

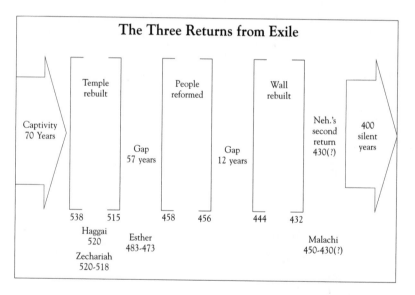

The Three Returns from Exile

Captivity 70 Years

Temple rebuilt — Haggai 520, Zechariah 520-518

Gap 57 years

People reformed — Esther 483-473

Gap 12 years

Wall rebuilt

Neh.'s second return 430(?) — Malachi 450-430(?)

400 silent years

538   515   458   456   444   432

1. Bruce Wilkinson and Kenneth Boa, *Talk Thru the Old Testament*, vol. 1 of *Talk Thru the Bible* (Nashville, Tenn.: Thomas Nelson Publishers, 1983), p. 120.

Author and Literary Characteristics

Although Ezra is not specifically named as the author, the first-person narrative from chapter 7 onward suggests that he indeed wrote the book. Also, the vivid, detailed descriptions in the latter part of the book require a writer who had firsthand knowledge of the events.

The book of Ezra is similar in many ways to the Chronicles, which leads some scholars to conclude that Ezra wrote 1 and 2 Chronicles as well. For example, the temple is a major theme in Ezra—its physical condition pictures the people's spiritual condition. Records, especially lists, also play an important part in Ezra and the Chronicles. Ezra provides a list of returning family heads and towns, records of royal correspondence, and an inventory of temple articles. Like the censuses, genealogies, and accounts of the kings in the Chronicles, the detailed information in Ezra shows how intimately and thoroughly God chose, protected, and guided His people.

Overall Structure of Ezra

The main events in the lives of the returnees, and the men who oversaw these events, form the two main divisions of the book. Chapters 1–6 focus on the *construction* of the temple under Zerubbabel's leadership. Chapters 7–10 emphasize the *reformation* of the people under the guidance of Ezra.

Construction (Ezra 1–6)

As we noted earlier, Ezra begins where 2 Chronicles left off—with the edict of Cyrus, king of Persia.

Proclamation and Preparation

Now in the first year of Cyrus king of Persia, in order to fulfill the word of the Lord by the mouth of Jeremiah,[2] the Lord stirred up the spirit of Cyrus king of Persia, so that he sent a proclamation throughout all his kingdom, and also put it in writing, saying, "Thus says Cyrus king of Persia, 'The

2. See Jeremiah 25:8–14; 29:10–14.

5

Lord, the God of heaven, has given me all the kingdoms of the earth, and He has appointed me to build Him a house in Jerusalem, which is in Judah. Whoever there is among you of all His people, may his God be with him! Let him go up to Jerusalem which is in Judah, and rebuild the house of the Lord, the God of Israel; He is the God who is in Jerusalem.'" (Ezra 1:1–3)

Talk about the sovereignty of God! Here's a pagan king who inherits somewhere around two to three million Jewish captives from his predecessor. By now they have bought homes, opened businesses, and blended into society. These Hebrews represent a lot of labor and tax income for Persia. Yet Cyrus says, "Go home; rebuild."

Notice who jumps into action first: the "heads of fathers' households of Judah and Benjamin and the priests and the Levites" (v. 5). That's significant. Though assimilated into a pagan culture, the Jews had maintained their tribal structure, including the role of priests and Levites. Mere tradition? For some, perhaps. But for many, the continuance of that structure was a sign of faith that they would once again return to the land God had allotted to them and worship Him in the way He had commanded.

Some can't wait to start the journey. Others stay but donate precious metals and livestock for the reinstitution of temple worship. Even Cyrus makes a contribution! He gives back all the temple articles that had been carted off by Nebuchadnezzar in 586 B.C. (vv. 6–11).

The First Wave

The first group, then, sets out for Jerusalem in the year 538 B.C. The list of returnees and cities in chapter 2 may hardly seem worth taking the time to read. But it's important for several reasons.

> First, the Lord knows His people personally. The covenant relation between the Lord and His people is a bond of intimate friendship. Second, common people are vital to the accomplishing of God's redemptive plan. . . . Not only are the religious and political leaders important in rebuilding the house of God, but so are the common people. In fact, "the rest of the people" contributed more to the rebuilding than did "the heads of the fathers' houses" and the

6

governor (Neh. 7:70–72). Third, the enumeration resembles those found in Numbers and Joshua (Num. 1; 26; Josh. 18; 19). As the Lord formed the covenant community following the Exodus from Egypt, so He re-creates it following the return from Babylon.[3]

The first name on the list, appropriately, is Zerubbabel (2:2), the governor who supervises the reconstruction of the temple (see Hag. 1:1). He is the grandson of Jehoiachin, the next-to-last king of Judah (see 1 Chron. 3:18–19). What better man to lead the exiles out of Babylon and back to Jerusalem than a descendent of King David, to whom God had promised an enduring kingdom.

Rebuilding Underway

Once in Jerusalem, the people go to work on the central feature of the temple—the altar (Ezra 3:1–3). This is significant because the altar not only shows their renewed commitment to the Mosaic Law, but through the atoning sacrifices, the people are reinstituting intimate fellowship with their holy, loving God. With the covenant sacrifices and festivals reestablished (vv. 4–6), laying the temple's foundation gets underway (vv. 7–10). Upon its completion, the people praise God in song:

> "For He is good, for His lovingkindness is upon Israel forever." (v. 11a)

Some of those seeing this new foundation were alive the day Nebuchadnezzar burned the temple to the ground. As they were carted off to Babylon, the last thing they saw was smoke rising from the temple ruins. Now they have returned from Jerusalem to watch the house of God rise from the ashes.

Overcome with emotion, some weep openly, while others shout praises to God. Trumpets blare and cymbals crash. The God of the Ages is about to take His place again as the focal point of the Jewish community.

Every work of God, however, draws the attention of the Enemy. The "enemies of Judah and Benjamin" try to sabotage the project by infiltrating the ranks of the builders (4:1–3). When that doesn't

3. New Geneva Study Bible, ed. R. C. Sproul, Bruce Waltke, Moisés Silva, and others (Nashville, Tenn.: Thomas Nelson Publishers, 1995), p. 649, note on 2:1–70.

work, they try to frighten the builders—even hiring "counselors" to frustrate and discourage the people (vv. 4–5).

This harassment continues through the reign of four Persian kings—Cyrus, Cambyses, Smerdis, and Darius I. In fact, building comes to a halt for fifteen years (535–520 B.C.). Finally, under the reign of Darius in 515 B.C., the temple is completed—with a kick start from the prophets Haggai and Zechariah (4:24–6:22; especially 5:1; 6:14; and the books by the prophets' names).

Chapter 4 of Ezra is a little hard to follow because it doesn't flow chronologically. It helps to see 4:1–5 and 4:24–6:22 as one unit that explains the process of building the temple from its beginning under Cyrus to its completion under Darius I. Inserted in the middle of this section is 4:6–23, which describes future hostility against the returnees, who tried to rebuild Jerusalem's walls, under Xerxes and Artaxerxes. It's as though Ezra wanted to show that the hostility begun during the temple's building continued even after the temple was completed—a somber reminder, perhaps, that the joy of worshiping and serving God is always accompanied by Satan's attempts to spoil it.

Satan, however, cannot thwart the plans of God. Darius I searches the royal archives and discovers the original edict of Cyrus. He honors it and commands that temple construction proceed with his approval and financial assistance. Finally, twenty-three years after the first wave returned to Jerusalem, the completed temple is dedicated with celebration and the first Passover since King Josiah's time, more than a hundred years earlier.

The presence of the temple, though, never guarantees the piety of the people. Over the next several decades, the remnant starts to slip away from the Lord. The people, including many of the priests, marry foreign women. Determined not to let His people again adopt the lifestyle of surrounding godless nations, God sends a true man of the Word to Jerusalem to confront the people with His commandments. As God has used stones and timber to rebuild His temple, He will use the preaching of Ezra to rebuild His people.

Reformation (Ezra 7–10)

In chapter 7, Artaxerxes is king. The year is 458 B.C.—eighty years after the first wave of exiles returned to Jerusalem under Zerubbabel to rebuild the temple. The second, smaller exodus from Babylon (about 1,800 people) is led by Ezra,

Ezr a scribe skilled in the law of Moses, which the Lord God of Israel had given; and the king granted him all he requested because the hand of the Lord his God was upon him. (v. 6)

Why Ezra? Speaking from God's sovereign perspective, he is God's choice. We're told three times in chapter 7 that the hand of the Lord is upon him (vv. 6, 9, 28). But God doesn't choose people without equipping them. Ezra is equipped; he is steeped in the Scriptures.

For Ezra had set his heart to study the law of the Lord, and to practice it, and to teach His statutes and ordinances in Israel. (v. 10)

Ezra has "set his heart," that is, made it his purpose, to know, then live, and *then* teach the Scriptures. It was possible for a scribe to copy the Scriptures, be exposed to them every day, and still not have them touch his life. Ezra isn't satisfied with simply stockpiling knowledge. He wants his life to reflect all he takes in. And he wants others to learn and change as well. He longs to see his kinsmen do more than return physically to Jerusalem. He wants them to return spiritually to the Lord.

So, when Artaxerxes decrees that he return to Jerusalem and teach the Word to the people, Ezra the priest-scribe assembles a company of priests, Levites, and "other sons of Israel" (chap. 7). Chapter 8 lists those who returned with Ezra.

When he arrives, Ezra learns that many of the returnees, including several leaders, have intermarried with surrounding pagan nations. Ezra's response is a good model for us to follow when confronting sin. First, he grieves (9:3). Then he confesses the sin to God, including himself as one who has fallen short of God's standards (vv. 6–15). Next, he publicly calls the people to repent and covenant with God to change (10:10–11). Finally, he follows through to make sure the people keep their word (vv. 2–17). Ezra's book closes with a list of all those who have taken foreign wives, an indication that sin has been exposed and dealt with (vv. 18–44).

Through Ezra's courageous and compassionate confrontation, the water of God's Word has once again fallen on the parched hearts of His people. Now all Jerusalem is awash in revival.

Only one thing remains—to rebuild the wall around the city. For that project, God has in mind a Jew serving in the court of

King Artaxerxes. His name is Nehemiah, and he will lead the third wave of remnants from Babylon to the Holy City, Jerusalem.

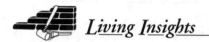 *Living Insights*

The parallel between rebuilding the temple and rebuilding people is unmistakable in Ezra. Both projects fall under the sovereign control of God. Both involve community rather than isolation. Both meet resistance. Both require time and commitment. Both have the Word of God at the center. And both bring glory and honor to God.

Where are you in the spiritual building process? Just laying the foundation? Well into the project? Has resistance or opposition put things on hold? Maybe you're just coming out of captivity and thinking about how to start fresh. How would you describe where you are now in your spiritual life?

_____

_____

_____

_____

What does God's protection of His people during captivity and after their release tell you about His commitment to maintain a relationship with us?

_____

_____

_____

Most of the Jews chose to stay in Babylon. What does that tell you about following the majority on spiritual matters?

_____

_____

_____

What do the decrees of Cyrus (Ezra 1:2–4), Darius (6:3–12), and Artaxerxes (7:12–26) say about God's remembering us and working for our good, even during the darkest days?

_____

_____

_____

What does Ezra's commitment to the Scriptures and His involvement in the spiritual restoration of the returnees say about our need to know what God says in His Word about living?

_____

_____

_____

The spiritual building process is just that—a process. The project won't be complete until we get to heaven. In the meantime, though, people all around us are watching the spiritual building go up. We, "as living stones, are being built up as a spiritual house for a holy priesthood, to offer up spiritual sacrifices acceptable to God through Jesus Christ" (1 Pet. 2:5).

Yes, we're always under construction. But the project is in the hands of the Master Builder. That means the building will one day be complete. And it will stand forever.

Chapter 2

NEHEMIAH: SOFTHEARTED HARD HAT

A Survey of Nehemiah

I f you grew up in the church, you probably remember the first time you saw your pastor outside of Sunday morning worship.

Most likely, he was doing something surprisingly normal, like standing in the express line at the grocery store, a gallon of milk dangling from one arm and a loaf of bread clutched under the other.

There he was, looking downright mortal in his faded Levis, battle-scarred tennis shoes, and University of Texas T-shirt. No tie, no flowing robe, no podium. Suddenly you realized that the thunder-voiced preacher who loomed over the congregation each Sunday was just a regular guy who shops and eats like the rest of us.

Spiritual leaders don't always look like we expect them to, do they? Though it's tempting to confine them in stereotypical strait-jackets, most spiritual leaders defy rigid categorization. They come in all shapes, sizes, personalities, and professions. Some, believe it or not, aren't even Sunday-morning preachers.

Take Nehemiah, for example. A contemporary of Ezra, Nehemiah was a versatile leader. He served in the courts of Persian royalty and eventually governed Judah. Of all the hats Nehemiah wore, however, he is best known for donning a construction hard hat and rebuilding the wall around his beloved Jerusalem.

Nehemiah's dedication and dependence on God teach us that, no matter what we do, we labor under the sovereign hand of our Lord. God provides us with a passion to participate in His work, and gives us the strength and resources to perform it. When we take on with passion and dedication the tasks He has given us, we get the satisfaction of a job well done, and God gets the glory.

A Sequel to Ezra

As we said in the previous lesson, the books of Ezra and Nehemiah were considered a single unit for centuries. Authors Bruce Wilkinson and Kenneth Boa further explain the relationship between the two books:

NEHEMIAH

	Cupbearer to the King	Builder of the Wall	Governor of the People	
	Prayer — May I? You may!	"So the wall was completed . . . in 52 days." (6:15)	Scripture found (7:5) read (8:3–7) explained (8:8)	Lives changed (8:1–3, 9; 10:28–31)	Nation confronted and cleansed (13:10–30) **Prayer**
	CHAPTERS 1:1–2:10	*CHAPTERS 2:11–6:19*	*CHAPTERS 7–13*	
Location	Susa, Persia		Jerusalem in Palestine	
Focus	Leadership of a man		Revival of a nation	
Subject	Burden	Project	Scriptures	Reforms
Difficulties	The King	Enemies	Tradition	Compromise
Victories	Release	Accomplishment	Obedience	Changes
Theme	Nehemiah's trust in the covenant-keeping God			
Key Verses	6:15–16; 8:8–10; 9			
Christ in Nehemiah	Suggested in Nehemiah, who leaves an exalted position to identify with the plight of his people and lead them into restoration. Pictured in Nehemiah's prayerful dependence on God.			

While Ezra deals primarily with the religious restoration of Judah, Nehemiah is concerned with Judah's political and geographical restoration. The first seven chapters are devoted to the rebuilding of Jerusalem's walls because Jerusalem was the spiritual and political center of Judah. Without walls, Jerusalem could hardly be considered a city at all. As governor, Nehemiah also established firm civil authority. Ezra and Nehemiah worked together to build the people spiritually and morally so that the restoration would be complete.[1]

Overall Structure

The structure of Nehemiah closely resembles that of Ezra, dividing into two main sections: the physical construction of the wall (chaps. 1–6) and the spiritual restoration of the people (chaps. 7–13).

We can also look at this book through the lens of the man himself and the roles he performed: Nehemiah as cupbearer to the king (1:1–2:10), rebuilder of the wall (2:11–6:19), and governor of the people (7:1–13:31). Three roles. One man. One heart for God.

Cupbearer to the King (Neh. 1:1–2:10)

Like Ezra, Nehemiah was born in captivity under the rule of a pagan king. As the book opens, we find Nehemiah serving in Susa, the winter capital of Persia, as cupbearer to King Artaxerxes.

The job of cupbearer is more important than it sounds. The king's very life rested in the hands (and in the palate) of the cupbearer, who tasted the king's wine to make sure it wasn't poisoned. Only the most honest, trustworthy, and discreet individuals would have been chosen for that post.

Bad News from Home

Though born and raised in Persia, Nehemiah knew his heritage and history well enough to have emotional ties to Judah. That's why he asked the men who recently visited Jerusalem about the condition

---

1. Bruce Wilkinson and Kenneth Boa, *Talk Thru the Old Testament*, vol. 1 of *Talk Thru the Bible* (Nashville, Tenn.: Thomas Nelson Publishers, 1983), p. 125.

of the city and the remnant living there. The report was dismal:

> And they said to me, "The remnant there in the
> province who survived the captivity are in great
> distress and reproach, and the wall of Jerusalem is
> broken down and its gates are burned with fire."
> (Neh. 1:3)

Jerusalem, remember, had been destroyed by Nebuchadnezzar in 586 B.C. The first wave of returnees (under Zerubbabel in 538 B.C.) rebuilt the temple and had begun repairing the city walls (Ezra 4:12). The enemies of Judah, however, managed to influence Artaxerxes to stop the work by decree earlier in his reign (Ezra 4:21).

Jerusalem lay desolate and unprotected, a smoldering shadow of its past glory. The news broke Nehemiah's heart. He was nine hundred miles away from the city he loved and could do nothing. Or could he?

Prayer: The First Course of Action

After Nehemiah mourned, he prayed—to the only One who could fully understand his grief and provide a way to help his kinsmen. In his prayer, Nehemiah reflected on God's covenant faithfulness and confessed the sins of his people, including his own. Only after doing these did he ask for God's help.

> "O Lord, I beseech Thee, may Thine ear be attentive
> to the prayer of Thy servant and the prayer of Thy
> servants who delight to revere Thy name, and make
> Thy servant successful today, and grant him com-
> passion before this man." (Neh. 1:11; compare
> Solomon's similar prayer at the temple dedication
> in 1 Kings 8:23–53)

"This man," of course, was Artaxerxes.

Fear and Boldness before the King

Nehemiah's distress over Jerusalem apparently showed on his face, for when he handed the king his wine, Artaxerxes asked, "Why are you so gloomy?" The question made Nehemiah "very much afraid" (2:2). Why? In Persian culture, the king required everyone to display a happy disposition in his presence. You could lose your life for having a bad day. Also, years earlier, Artaxerxes had halted construction in Jerusalem. To return and rebuild the wall,

Nehemiah would be, in essence, asking him to reverse that decree. No wonder he was afraid.

Nevertheless, Nehemiah recognized this moment as the opportunity to present his petition before the king. He began by explaining the reason for his sadness (v. 3), and would you believe . . .

> the king said to me, "What would you request?" So I prayed to the God of heaven. (v. 4)

No punishment! Just interest. So Nehemiah prayed on the spot. Actually, he had been praying and planning for four months.[2] He knew how long the trip would take. He needed royal letters of passage through neighboring provinces. And he needed the king's approval to procure building materials.

Confidently, yet respectfully, Nehemiah then asked for all these things. And the king granted each request, because the hand of God was on Nehemiah (v. 8).

Builder of the Wall (Neh. 2:11–6:19)

Once in Jerusalem, and after examining the wall himself, Nehemiah rallied the people to start rebuilding. The opposition, however, was also rallying—they saw rebuilding as a threat against their power (though they couched it as the Jews rebelling against the king) and an opportunity for the Jews to regain their long-lost prominence and identity (2:19).

Determination against Opposition

Nehemiah, though, wasn't intimidated, and chapter 3 shows the great detail and organization with which the work proceeded. Gates were repaired, doors hung, holes patched, and gold replaced. The thread of purpose and pride patched together people from all social classes—priest worked beside politician, craftsman next to commoner. This was a project for the whole remnant.

In chapter 4, the opposition—Sanballat the Horonite, governor of Samaria, and Tobiah the Ammonite, possibly governor of Transjordan[3]—tried to stop the work with taunts and ridicule.

---

2. Nehemiah heard the sad news about Jerusalem in Chislev, our November-December (1:1), and he spoke with the king about it in Nisan, our March-April (2:1).

3. See Edwin Yamauchi and Ronald Youngblood, "Nehemiah," in *The NIV Study Bible*, ed. Kenneth L. Barker and others (Grand Rapids, Mich.: Zondervan Bible Publishers, 1985), pp. 695–96, note on Nehemiah 2:10.

When that didn't work, they threatened to use force. God's people prayed for His protection, and then Nehemiah posted guards around the wall and encouraged the people that God would fight for them. The builders kept going, and "each wore his sword girded at his side as he built" (v. 18).

Opposition, though, wasn't limited to the outside. Inside the walls, strife threatened to divide the Jewish community. In order to survive, many Jews had to borrow money from their fellow countrymen. Those loaning the money were apparently charging excessive interests, making it necessary for the borrowers to sell their homes and businesses, even sell their sons and daughters into slavery (5:1–5).

Knowing the wall (and the nation) couldn't rise with this kind of infighting, Nehemiah confronted the lenders with their abuses. In response, they returned their ill-gotten gain (vv. 6–13).

Nehemiah modeled what he asked. As governor of Judah—a post to which he was appointed sometime during the building of the wall—he was entitled to a food allowance taken from the people. He refused it, however, paying for the entertaining of dignitaries out of his own pocket (vv. 14–19; compare 2 Thess. 3:8–9).

Finished at Last!

Though the inside conflicts ceased, the outside opposition continued. Sanballat, Tobiah, and others relentlessly tried to entrap Nehemiah and even ruin his reputation (Neh. 6:1–14). But the builder kept at his task until "the wall was completed on the twenty-fifth of the month Elul, in fifty-two days" (v. 15).

While some outside resistance continued, the nations took notice that God had helped His people complete the task.

The walls took fifty-two days to rebuild. Rebuilding the people, however, would take much longer.

Governor of the People (Neh. 7–13)

After hanging the last doors on the gates and organizing the logistics of access to the city, Nehemiah turned his attention to improving community life (7:1–4).

He started by perusing the list of people who had come from Babylon to Jerusalem under Zerubbabel (vv. 5–73a). Once he had a feel for who was living in Jerusalem, he assembled them all at the Water Gate for a reading of the Law (7:73b–8:1). And guess who the reader was.

Ezra Reads the Law

Remember Ezra? He arrived in Jerusalem fourteen years before Nehemiah. During that time, he had been instructing people in the Law of God. With the wall now completed, he was called on once again to open the Scriptures.

As he read, the people responded in worship (8:6). Priests and Levites circulated among the crowd to explain the Law further, and the people wept aloud—possibly because of their remorse over past disobedience (v. 9). Nehemiah, however, reminded the people that this was a day of celebration; God had been faithful to forgive and restore them, just as He had promised so long ago (see Deut. 30:1–10). "Do not be grieved," he told them, "for the joy of the Lord is your strength" (Neh. 8:10b).

Confession and Recommitment

Upon hearing the Word, the people confessed their sins and reflected on the greatness and faithfulness of God, who had protected His people through the ages.

Chapter 9 records a historical reflection on God's love, patience, mercy, and judgment extended to the people of Israel from God's covenant with Abraham to their present day in Persia-ruled Judah. It's Scriptures' own overview of itself, covering Genesis through 2 Kings.

Vowing not to repeat the mistakes of their ancestors, the people made a public commitment to follow God's Law (9:38–10:39).

Geographic Distribution of the People

With the walls completed and the people committed to the Lord, Jerusalem was now inhabitable and ready to function again as the Holy City. The leaders of the people resided in Jerusalem, and lots were drawn to decide how the rest of the people would be distributed (chap. 11).

The first half of chapter 12 reviews the priestly lineage of Israel, most likely to affirm the connection with the order of worship David had instituted. This link to the king after God's own heart, "David the man of God" (v. 24), and to Israel's glory days would have encouraged the original readers that they were following in footsteps pleasing to God.

Dedication of the Wall

With music, singing, pageantry, and worship, the Jews celebrated the wall's completion. After the priests and Levites had purified themselves, the people, the gates, and the walls, two choirs marched on top of the wall around the city in a great scene of antiphonal worship. The enemies who had earlier mocked the Jews for trying to rebuild the wall must have stood aghast at this revelry.

This dedication, though, wasn't an opportunity to flaunt their triumph. Rather, it was a time to bask in God's goodness and set apart their re-formed community for God's use. Appropriately, all the pageantry moved into the temple, culminating in generous sacrifices and rejoicing heard "from afar" (v. 43).

Nehemiah's Later Reforms

Some time after the completion of the wall, Nehemiah returned to Persia to serve again under Artaxerxes (13:6). But he would come back to Jerusalem again, as Gene A. Getz explains:

> While he was gone [from Jerusalem] some rather startling changes took place in Judah, changes involving serious violations of the Mosaic Law. When Nehemiah once again returned to Judah (perhaps around 430 or later), he faced a task that in some respects must have been even more difficult than rebuilding the wall.[4]

Among Nehemiah's reforms:

- While Nehemiah was in Persia, Tobiah, the Jews' old enemy, had arranged to use temple storage rooms set apart for tithes and offerings to store his own possessions! Nehemiah threw this Ammonite intruder out of the temple, in accordance with God's Law (v. 8; see also Deut. 23:3; Neh. 13:1–2).

- The people had stopped tithing, thus neglecting the temple and the Levites. So Nehemiah not only prompted the people to tithe again, he oversaw the monetary distribution (vv. 10–14).

- He discovered that people were working on the Sabbath, so he closed off the city to business on that sacred day (vv. 15–22).

4. Gene A. Getz, "Nehemiah," in *The Bible Knowledge Commentary*, Old Testament edition, ed. John F. Walvoord and Roy B. Zuck (Wheaton, Ill.: Scripture Press Publications, Victor Books, 1985), p. 694.

- The people had also violated their commitment to not intermarry—even the priests were practicing this sin. He confronted them, even manhandled some of them, and put a stop to it (vv. 23–29).

A spiritual leader who hits people and pulls out their hair? Not exactly a model for local church ministry. But let's face it. Sometimes radical holiness requires radical measures. And we should be willing to take them if our goal, like Nehemiah's, is serving and pleasing God.

> Remember me with favor, O my God. (v. 31b NIV; see also vv. 14, 22)

That's something we should all remember—no matter what kind of hat we wear.

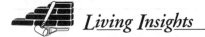 *Living Insights*

We can learn a lot from Nehemiah. How to analyze a difficult problem and craft a solution. How to stay true to our convictions and vision in the face of opposition. How to organize and motivate people around a common cause. How to stay with a task until it's done. How to delegate. Most importantly, though, we can learn how to pray.

Even with all his giftedness and obvious knack for administration and motivation, Nehemiah prayed. For he knew that, ultimately, success depended on God—the Author and Keeper of the "covenant of love" (Neh. 1:5 NIV).

Take a look at Nehemiah's prayer in 1:5–11. Can you identify the major sections of his prayer: reflection on God's character and work, confession of sin, request for success?

Which comes first?

Why do you suppose knowing who God is and what He has done for us is so important to our making requests of Him?

What does confession do for our relationship with God (see Lev. 26:40–45; Ps. 32:5)?

_____

_____

Does God want us to ask Him for things?

_____

_____

Here's a suggestion. Next time you pray, spend at least the first half of that time reflecting on who God is and what He has done. Then spend some time confessing your sins and thanking Him for His forgiveness. Finally, ask of Him. And be encouraged not only that He is capable of meeting your needs but that He delights in doing so.

So go ahead. Plan, think, manage, create, motivate. But above all, pray. For without our conscious dependence on God's power and wisdom, we may build our own little kingdom—but we'll miss the joy of building His (see also Neh. 4:7–14; 13:14; Matt. 6:33; 7:7–11; Phil. 4:6–7).

Chapter 3

ESTHER: BEAUTY
AND THE BEST

Survey of Esther

We often think of God's sovereignty on a grand scale—the sweeping act of Creation, the controlling and shaping of history. Frederick Buechner, though, tells us that we also experience God's sovereignty in smaller, more subtle ways.

> I think of a person I haven't seen or thought of for years, and ten minutes later I see her crossing the street. I turn on the radio to hear a voice reading the biblical story of Jael, which is the story that I have spent the morning writing about. A car passes me on the road, and its license plate consists of my wife's and my initials side by side. When you tell people stories like that, their usual reaction is to laugh. One wonders why.
>
> I believe that people laugh at coincidence as a way of relegating it to the realm of the absurd and of therefore not having to take seriously the possibility that there is a lot more going on in our lives than we either know or care to know. Who can say what it is that's going on, but I suspect that part of it, anyway, is that every once and so often we hear a whisper from the wings that goes something like this: "You've turned up in the right place at the right time. You're doing fine. Don't even think that you've been forgotten."[1]

God had certainly not forgotten His exiled people, enabling all who had a heart to return to go back and rebuild Jerusalem and their life as a holy nation. But what about those who, for one reason or another, stayed in Persia? Were they outside His care, His

---

1. Frederick Buechner, *Wishful Thinking: A Seeker's ABC*, rev. and exp. (San Francisco, Calif.: HarperSanFrancisco, 1993), pp. 17–18.

ESTHER

God's providence among his people during . . .

. . . Hard Times . . . Happy Times

Circumstance	King's Banquet	Haman's Edict	Queen's Courage	God's Deliverance	Mordecai's Edict	Jews' Rejoicing	Shalom!
	Honoring the kingdom		Urging of Mordecai	Mordecai honored		Enemies destroyed	
	Honoring the new queen		Approaching the King	Haman hanged		Feast established	
	CHAPTERS 1–2	CHAPTER 3	CHAPTERS 4–5	CHAPTERS 6–7	CHAPTER 8	CHAPTER 9	CHAPTER 10
	Threat and trust				Deliverance and praise		
Feasts	of the king		of the queen		of the nation		
Dates	483 B.C.						473 B.C.
Theme	The sovereign accomplishment of God's purposes through ordinary people and apparent coincidences						
Key Verses	4:12–16; 10:3						
Christ in Esther	Esther was an advocate for her people, even willing to die for them.						

23

memory? As the divine "coincidences" in the drama of Esther show, they were still safe in the palm of His hand.

Prologue

Before the players take the stage, let's learn a little about what the playwright had in mind.

Historical Background

The dramatic events recorded in Esther most likely took place between the exiles' first return under Zerubbabel and the second led by Ezra. The Persian king Xerxes I was ruling at the time (486–465 B.C.)—his name in Hebrew was Ahasuerus.

Notable Features

Esther's Hebrew name, Hadassah (2:7), means "myrtle." Her Persian name of Esther, though, means "star."[2] This is an appropriate name for a woman whose beauty and courage continue to shine brightly in the biblical record.

Though the author of Esther remains obscure, his dramatic devices leave a clear and lasting message. Raymond Dillard and Edwin Yamauchi explain.

> An outstanding feature of this book—one that has given rise to considerable discussion—is the complete absence of any explicit reference to God, worship, prayer, or sacrifice. This "secularity" has produced many detractors who have judged the book to be of little religious value. However, it appears that the author has deliberately refrained from mentioning God or any religious activity as a literary device to heighten the fact that it is God who controls and directs all the seemingly insignificant coincidences . . . that make up the plot and issue in deliverance for the Jews. God's sovereign rule is assumed at every point . . . , an assumption made all the more effective by the total absence of reference to him.[3]

2. Bruce Wilkinson and Kenneth Boa, Talk Thru the Old Testament, vol. 1 of Talk Thru the Bible (Nashville, Tenn.: Thomas Nelson Publishers, 1983), p. 131.

3. Raymond Dillard and Edwin Yamauchi, introduction to Esther, in The NIV Study Bible, ed. Kenneth Barker and others (Grand Rapids, Mich.: Zondervan Publishing House, 1985), p. 719.

Cast of Characters

King Ahasuerus, *also known as Xerxes I, king of Persia*
Queen Vashti, *soon-to-be ex-wife of Ahasuerus*
Mordecai, *an exiled Jew living in Persia, Esther's older cousin and guardian*
Esther, *Mordecai's beautiful ward, soon-to-be wife of Ahasuerus*
Haman, *the bad guy! Anti-Semitic and arrogant, this noble of the king plots the destruction of the Jews*

Act 1

As the lights dim and the curtain rises, we find ourselves at the palace in Susa, the winter capital of the Persian Empire.

Scene 1 (Esther 1)

The third year of Ahasuerus' reign, at least in the king's mind, has merited a banquet—make that a six-month long bash (Esther 1:1–4)! Not wanting anyone to be left out of the fun, Ahasuerus extends the gala for seven more days and invites "all the people who [are] present in Susa the capital, from the greatest to the least," to join the revelry in the garden court of his palace (v. 5).

The wine, in accord with the king's orders, flows freely (vv. 7–8).

Trouble begins when the king, by this time "merry with wine," commands his servants to tell the queen, who is giving her own, much smaller banquet, to come "display her beauty to the people and the princes" (v. 11). Sensibly, she says no, not wanting to parade herself before a drunken crowd. The king, not so merry at her refusal, consults with his "wise men" to determine a course of action. They counsel him to make an example of Queen Vashti so that "every man should be the master in his own house" (vv. 12–22). He issues an edict, and Vashti is banished from his presence, her royal position to be given to someone else.

Scene 2 (Esther 2)

Later, the king's temper passes and he realizes he misses Vashti.[4] His attendants suggest holding a beauty contest through which he can select her replacement (2:1–4). Among those chosen to

---

4. History tells us that after his banquet, Ahasuerus pursued a number of military campaigns against Greece that ended in disaster. It's possible, then, that several years had passed by the time he returned to Susa.

participate is Esther, who lives in Susa with her guardian-cousin, Mordecai (vv. 5–8).

Finding favor with the chief official of the king's harem, Esther receives special treatment. However, she keeps her identity as a Jew secret, per Mordecai's counsel (vv. 9–14). When she comes before the king, she wins his heart, and he proclaims her queen— celebrating with what else? Another banquet (vv. 15–18).

Mordecai, meanwhile, uncovers a plot to assassinate the king. He tells Esther, who informs Ahasuerus, and the plot is thwarted. The entire episode, including Mordecai's intervention, is recorded in the king's annals (vv. 19–23)—to come in handy at a future date.

Scene 3 (Esther 3)

From Mordecai's heroism the scene now shifts to the entrance of the villain, Haman, the Agagite.[5]

Recently promoted above all the other nobles, Haman takes offense when Mordecai, unlike the rest of the king's servants, refuses to bow down and pay homage to him. After learning Mordecai's nationality, Haman seeks to soothe his bruised ego by taking revenge—not just on Mordecai but on all the Jews (3:1–6).

He casts *pur*, or a lot, to determine the date for the genocide and then manipulates the king to declare a murderous edict. This decree, quickly dispatched by Persian post, will allow the people in every region of the empire to "destroy, to kill, and to annihilate all the Jews, both young and old, women and children, in one day" (v. 13). Ironically, that day is the thirteenth of Adar, the month before Passover. The lesson God taught Pharaoh so long ago about harming His people is lost on the vain, vengeful Haman.

Scene 4 (Esther 4)

While Ahasuerus and Haman toast their future success (3:15b), Mordecai and the whole Jewish community mourn their fate (4:1–3). Esther, however, isolated in the harem, learns only of Mordecai's distress and sends a messenger to find out what's going

---

5. Haman is linked here with one of Israel's worst enemies, the Amalekites. They were the first to attack Israel after the Exodus (Exod. 17:8–16), and the Lord promised He would "utterly blot out the memory of Amalek from under heaven" (v. 14). King Saul was supposed to fulfill this promise, but he failed to obey the Lord's command and spared their king, Agag's, life (1 Sam. 15). Interestingly, Mordecai is described as "the son of Jair, the son of Shimei, *the son of Kish*, a Benjamite" (Esther 2:5)—the other well-known son of Kish was King Saul (1 Sam. 9:1–2).

on. Mordecai tells the servant everything, sends a copy of the edict back with him, and adds a special message for Esther: Go before the king and plead for your people (vv. 4–8).

Going unsummoned before the king means death—unless he extends his golden scepter. Esther reminds Mordecai of this through her servant and adds that she hasn't been called before the king in thirty days. Mordecai and Esther's next exchange is the pivotal point of the book.

> Then Mordecai told them to reply to Esther, "Do not imagine that you in the king's palace can escape any more than all the Jews. For if you remain silent at this time, relief and deliverance will arise for the Jews from another place and you and your father's house will perish. And who knows whether you have not attained royalty for such a time as this?" Then Esther told them to reply to Mordecai, "Go, assemble all the Jews who are found in Susa, and fast for me; do not eat or drink for three days, night or day. I and my maidens also will fast in the same way. And thus I will go in to the king, which is not according to the law; and if I perish, I perish." (vv. 13–16)

Mordecai does as she asks (v. 17).

Scene 5 (Esther 5)

Risking her life, Esther stands uninvited before the king. Happily, he is pleased to see her and extends his scepter, eager to know and fulfill whatever she might request. She asks only that he and Haman will come to her banquet that day. At the banquet, she further piques the king's interest by putting off an answer to his questions until he and Haman come to another banquet the next day (5:1–8).

Haman, bloated on royal food and pride, encounters the still unbowed Mordecai on the way home and becomes enraged that the Jew will not grovel before him. When he gets home, he boasts about his status with the royal couple but pouts about Mordecai. His wife and friends try to lift his spirits by suggesting he hang Mordecai—on a gallows seventy-five feet high—tomorrow morning. Haman likes the idea, and has a gallows built (vv. 9–14).

Scene 6 (Esther 6)

By another divine "coincidence," King Ahasuerus has insomnia that night. Hoping to read himself to sleep, he orders his book of records brought in—and finds the account of how Mordecai saved his life (see 2:19–23). When he learns that Mordecai has never been rewarded for this, Ahasuerus asks for whichever advisor is in the court—and it just happens to be Haman (6:1–5).

When the king asks Haman, "What is to be done for the man whom the king desires to honor?" (v. 6b), Haman, thinking the king's going to honor him, devises a highly flattering plan. In a twist of fate, Ahasuerus orders Haman to honor Mordecai with his plan; afterwards, Haman returns home disgraced, his wife foretelling his doom (vv. 7–13).

Scene 7 (Esther 7)

Rushed to Esther's banquet, Haman breaks into a cold sweat. When the king asks Esther her request, she asks for her life and exposes the plot to destroy her people (7:1–4). When King Ahasuerus asks "who would presume to do thus," Esther answers, "A foe and an enemy, is this wicked Haman!" (vv. 5–6). Furious, the king stalks out of the banquet but returns to mistake Haman's begging Esther for his life as an assault on the queen (vv. 7–8). With swift punishment, the king has Haman hung on the gallows he built for Mordecai (vv. 9–10).

Act 2

With Haman gone, the Jews' troubles are over . . . or are they?

Scene 1 (Esther 8)

Since the law of the Medes and Persians cannot be revoked, the decree Haman devised to annihilate the Jews still stands. Mordecai, however, now promoted to Haman's place of honor, comes up with another strategy to save his people. He arranges with the king to publish a second edict, one that will allow the Jews in all the provinces to "assemble and defend their lives" (8:1–14). The garments of mourning are cast off, and "for the Jews there [is] light and gladness and joy and honor" (v. 16).

Scene 2 (Esther 9)

When Adar the thirteenth arrives, the Jews rout their enemies (9:1–9, 16). Haman's ten sons perish and are displayed on their father's gallows the next day (vv. 10–14). At Esther's request, the edict is extended an additional day in Susa, and the Jews again destroy those who hate them (v. 15).

To commemorate their deliverance from their enemies, Mordecai institutes the Feast of Purim—*purim* is plural for "lots," a reference to Haman's method of choosing the day of the Jews' destruction (vv. 16–32). In this way, the Jews are to remember this

> month which was turned for them from sorrow into gladness and from mourning into a holiday; that they should make them days of feasting and rejoicing and sending portions of food to one another and gifts to the poor. . . . These days were to be remembered and celebrated throughout every generation, every family, every province, and every city; and these days of Purim were not to fail from among the Jews, or their memory fade from their descendants. (vv. 22, 28)

Epilogue

Like Joseph and Daniel before him (see Gen. 41:37–40; Dan. 2:48; 6:1–3), Mordecai was promoted so that he was second only to the king himself (10:3a). And the writer of Esther, in giving the reasons for Mordecai's greatness, tacitly affirms God's care for His people.

> [Mordecai was esteemed because he was] one who sought the good of his people and one who spoke for the welfare of his whole nation. (v. 3b)

Living Insights

The book of Esther shows that God's sovereign direction, also called providence, doesn't require high visibility. It is present in many little, seemingly insignificant things—like beauty contests and insomnia. Things that, when the tale's all told, seem less like coincidences than gracefully orchestrated events.

But even when God arranges circumstances, He expects us to play our part.

Merely being at the right place at the right time is not enough; opportunity does not equal victory. A lot hinges on our response, as Mordecai reminded Esther. Look again at his words in Esther 4:13–14. What do they tell you?

_____

_____

_____

How do Mordecai's words, especially in verse 14, relate to King Saul's failure in 1 Samuel 15? Who ultimately delivered God's people from the Amalekites and Agag's descendants (remember Esther 3:1)?

_____

_____

_____

When our responses are fear-driven or stem from self-interest or dullness toward God, we can close ourselves off from His plans, as King Saul would attest. However, when we respond with integrity, courage, and faith, we are allowed to participate with God in turning sovereign "coincidences" into victory, as Esther's story gives witness to.

God's sovereignty, His "coincidences," always have a purpose. Stretched like a banner across the book of Esther is His message: I care. He cares for His people's well-being, desiring to turn "sorrow into gladness . . . mourning into a holiday" (Esther 9:22). Or as Isaiah put it:

> To grant those who mourn in Zion,
> Giving them a garland instead of ashes,
> The oil of gladness instead of mourning,
> The mantle of praise instead of a spirit of faint-
> ing. (Isa. 61:3a)

Esther and Mordecai cared about what God cares about—His people. And so did Christ, to the point of being stretched like a banner of love on the cross.

Do we?

Chapter 4

JOB: MAGNIFICENT MAN OF MISERY

A Survey of Job

> Real faith cannot be reduced to spiritual bromides
> and merchandised in success stories. It is refined in
> the fires and the storms of pain.
> —Eugene Peterson[1]

Suffering is part of living. Most of us acknowledge that, but we sometimes strain to see suffering's value. It seems unnatural, even masochistic, to embrace pain as a divine tool that hones our faith or as a lens through which we can see God more clearly. And it's especially hard to embrace when it's undeserved, when it comes out of nowhere.

We can understand being punished for a crime or paying for abusing our health. But when suffering blindsides us, we want reasons, don't we? We search for a connection between the life we're leading and the pain we're experiencing.

That's why we're drawn to the story of Job, a blameless man who "was doing everything right when suddenly everything went wrong."[2] Job lost more in the blink of an eye—family, possessions, position, health—than most of us will lose in a lifetime. If anyone ever had cause to ask, "Why me?" it was Job.

Some suffering will always remain a mystery to us. But in Job's poetic profile of pain, we find that God reveals Himself in the midst of it. And often, while groping for the *whys* of suffering, we instead find the *Who*—our living, loving Lord.

Poetic Suffering

With the book of Job, we enter the poetical section of Scripture, consisting of Job, Psalms, Proverbs, Ecclesiastes, and Song of Solomon. Job is actually one long Hebrew poem held together by two bookends of prose.

---

1. Eugene H. Peterson, *The Message: Job* (Colorado Springs, Colo.: NavPress, 1996), p. 8.

2. Peterson, *The Message*, p. 6.

JOB

	Introduction to the Suffering	Words of Job (Eyes on Self)	Discussion of the Suffering — Words of Three Friends (Eyes on Humanity)			Correction in the Suffering — Words of Elihu (Eyes on Yahweh)	Correction in the Suffering — Words of Yahweh (Emphasis on Sovereignty)	Submission under the Suffering	Restoration from the Suffering
	Scene 1 Job's purity and prosperity **Scene 2** Satan's proposition and Yahweh's permission **Scene 3** Satan's persecution and Job's patience **Scene 4** Satan's persistence and Yahweh's permission **Scene 5** Poverty and plagues	Curses birth Curses life	Eliphaz → Job Zophar Bildad	Eliphaz → Job Zophar Bildad	Eliphaz → Job Bildad Job's Monologue	To Job To three friends To Job		Job's admission Job's confession	Yahweh's anger with the three friends Yahweh's blessing on Job
	CHAPTERS 1–2	CHAPTER 3	CHAPTERS 4–14	CHAPTERS 15–21	CHAPTERS 22–31	CHAPTERS 32–37	CHAPTERS 38–41	CHAPTER 42:1–6	CHAPTER 42:7–17
Key Sections	Historical		Theological/Philosophical			Logical	Revelational	Confessional	Historical
Key People	Job, Yahweh, and Satan		Job, Eliphaz, Bildad, Zophar			Elihu	Yahweh	Job	Yahweh, Job, and the three friends
Key Sayings	"Have you considered my servant Job?" (1:8)		"… then Job … Eliphaz … Bildad … Zophar answered"			God does "great things which we cannot comprehend" (37:5)	"Whatever is under the whole heaven is Mine" (41:11)	"Therefore I retract, and I repent in dust and ashes" (42:6)	"The Lord blessed the latter days of Job more than his beginning" (42:12)
Main Theme	God's sovereignty and humanity's struggle in the midst of suffering								
Christ in Job	Job's cry for a Mediator (9:33; 33:23–24) and his faith in a Redeemer (19:25–27) foreshadow the intersessory work of Christ.								

Fully one-third of the Hebrew Bible was written in poetry.[3] Who says revelation is a boring list of do's and don'ts? It is rich spiritual truth, artfully poured through human experience and emotion.

Ancient Hebrew poetry resembles the poetry found in many other languages. It's rich with images, has concise and concrete expressions, and artistically presents the human experience. Hebrew poetry, however, lacks both rhyme and meter. Instead, it is characterized by parallelism, a "rhyming" of ideas.

In parallelism, an idea is stated, then followed by a similar statement that echoes, opposes, or completes the previous idea. Job, for example, said,

> "Let the day perish on which I was to be born,
> And the night which said, 'A boy is conceived.'"
> (Job 3:3)

Two lines that eloquently reveal one desperate emotion: "I wish I had never been born."

We'll look more at Hebrew poetry when we come to the Psalms. Right now, let's consider some background on Job.

Author

No one knows for sure who wrote the book of Job. Suggestions range from Job himself, to Elihu (one of Job's counselors), Moses, Solomon, Isaiah, Hezekiah, and Ezra.

The detailed and lengthy conversations in Job suggest the author was an eyewitness. Since Job lived 140 years after the events in the book (42:16), he or another eyewitness could have compiled it during this time. Job, of course, would not have recorded the account of his own death.

Date

The date of the book's writing is also a mystery, but we have some hints about when the events occurred. Job's long life (possibly two hundred years or more), his accumulation of livestock as a sign of wealth, his role as family priest, and his use of the patriarchal name for God (*Shaddai*) all suggest that Job lived during the patriarchal

---

3. Only five Old Testament books appear to have no poetry: Leviticus, Ruth, Ezra, Haggai, and Malachi. See Bruce Wilkinson and Kenneth Boa, *Talk Thru the Old Testament*, vol. 1 of *Talk Thru the Bible* (Nashville, Tenn.: Thomas Nelson Publishers, 1983), p. 139.

age, "perhaps between Genesis 11 and 12 or not long after the time of Abraham."[4]

If Job did live during the patriarchal age, and if the book was written shortly after the events took place, Job could be the oldest book in the Bible.

Structure of Job

The book's forty-two chapters take us from the beginning of Job's misery through his struggle to understand it, and, eventually, through his healing and restoration.

Introduction to Job's Suffering (Chaps. 1–2)

Job seems like such an unlikely candidate for suffering. He is "blameless, upright, fearing God, and turning away from evil" (1:1). His possessions are abundant, and his reputation great (v. 3). He cares about his family's spiritual condition, regularly offering sacrifices on behalf of his children (v. 5). And God delights in him (v. 8).

Unknown to Job, his integrity is being challenged in the courts of heaven. Satan, wanting to discredit Job and, in the process, God Himself, comes before the Lord and asks,

> "Does Job fear God for nothing? Hast Thou not made a hedge about him and his house and all that he has, on every side? Thou hast blessed the work of his hands, and his possessions have increased in the land. But put forth Thy hand now and touch all that he has; he will surely curse Thee to Thy face." (vv. 9–11)

Elmer B. Smick and Ronald Youngblood get to the heart of what Satan is trying to do here.

> Satan attempts with one crafty thrust both to assail God's beloved and to show up God as a fool. . . . He charges that Job's godliness is evil. The very godliness in which God takes delight is void of all integrity; . . . [Job] is righteous only because it pays.[5]

4. Wilkinson and Boa, *Talk Thru the Old Testament*, p. 144.

5. Elmer B. Smick and Ronald Youngblood, introduction to Job, in *The NIV Study Bible*, ed. Kenneth L. Barker and others (Grand Rapids, Mich.: Zondervan Bible Publishers, 1985), p. 732.

So God permits Satan to test His servant, and the Accuser wreaks havoc first on Job's family and possessions (vv. 13–19), then on his health (2:1–8).

Initially, Job accepts his plight and acknowledges God's right over his life. He even reprimands his wife for her suggestion that he "curse God and die" (2:9). As Job's suffering drags on, however, he grows more introspective and angry, imagining that God has become his enemy.

Discussion of Job's Suffering (Chaps. 3–31)

Now poor, dejected, and covered with painful boils, Job is joined by three friends who sit in silence with him for seven days (2:11–13). When Job finally speaks, he regrets the day of his birth (chap. 3). His three friends, responding to his lament, begin to speak in chapter 4.

This starts three cycles of debate about suffering. In each cycle, Job's friends present their explanations for Job's dilemma, and Job argues that their reasons are inadequate. High drama meets theological discourse as Job and his friends try to make sense out of suffering.

The First Cycle of Speeches (Chaps. 4–14)

Eliphaz

The first man to respond to Job is Eliphaz the Temanite (chaps. 4–5), probably the oldest member of the group, a man with a lot of living—and a lot of theology—under his belt. Yet, writes author Mike Mason,

> Eliphaz's noble bearing, his fatherly sincerity, and his adroit theologizing are not quite enough to cover up the underlying coldness of his heart. . . . For Job sits before him stripped of everything, his heart torn and exposed, his words desperate, his eyes wild and probing and pleading for comfort, and what does the gentle Eliphaz have to offer? Amidst all his smoothly eloquent talk, perhaps the gist of his entire message may be summed up by the stinging yet almost hidden little comment in 4:8: "As I have observed," he observes smugly, "those who sow trouble reap it."[6]

6. Mike Mason, *The Gospel According to Job* (Wheaton, Ill.: Good News Publishers, Crossway Books, 1994), p. 65.

35

Although Eliphaz obviously knows some things about God (he even claims to have received his revelation from a divine vision), he errs in his assumption that Job's suffering is God's discipline for sin. Though some indeed suffer for this reason, Eliphaz doesn't stop to consider that there may be another reason for Job's pain.

Job responds by reminding Eliphaz of the depth of his suffering. He rejects Eliphaz's argument, rebukes him for his insensitivity, demands to know how he has sinned, and vents his anger at God (chaps. 6–7).

Bildad

Next, Bildad the Shuhite chimes in:

> "How long will you say these things,
> And the words of your mouth be a mighty wind?
> Does God pervert justice
> Or does the Almighty pervert what is right?
> If your sons sinned against Him,
> Then He delivered them into the power of their
> transgression." (8:2–4)

How's that for compassion? Bildad, like Eliphaz, believes Job's suffering is the result of sin, and he urges repentance. But, where Eliphaz argued from personal experience ("according to what I have seen," 4:8), Bildad draws his hypothesis from history and tradition ("Please inquire of past generations," 8:8).

Job's answer to Bildad (chaps. 9–10)? "Tell me something I don't know." Job was aware that the wicked perish, but that wasn't his struggle. He wanted to know why *he* was suffering. Though Job desperately wanted to subpoena God for an answer, he felt hopeless trying to gain an audience with the Creator of the universe. After all, how can a mere mortal stand before such an all-powerful God?

Zophar

Enter Zophar the Naamathite (chap. 11), possibly the most caustic of the counselors. Mike Mason describes him this way:

> Zophar has obviously been chomping at the bit for
> a chance to put in his two cents' worth, and right
> off the bat he shows himself to be the sort of fellow
> who shoots first and asks questions later. In his crit-
> icism of Job he is not just blunt but insulting, calling

his friend a scoffer and a windbag (v. 3) and broadly accusing him of arrogant self-righteousness (v. 4).[7]

Zophar, like Eliphaz and Bildad, urges Job to repent and be restored. If Job remains unrepentant, Zophar surmises, he will perish.

All three counselors, though possessing some knowledge about God's righteousness and justice, fail to see that God sometimes has other reasons for human suffering than the punishment of sinners.

Job answers Zophar (chaps. 12–14) by jeering at his (and the others') alleged wisdom. They have told him nothing about God's power and wisdom that he does not already know. He vows to take his case directly to God, but then he rages at Him and sinks again into hopelessness.

The Second Cycle of Speeches (Chaps. 15–21)

In round two, Job's counselors continue their insistence that Job is suffering for sin. Now, however,

> they became more vicious than in the first round. Missing from these speeches is a call to repent. Added is a more hostile, hardened attitude. Underscoring the fate of the wicked, these arguers at the ash pile stressed the dangers facing the wicked (Eliphaz, chap. 15), the traps awaiting the wicked (Bildad, chap. 18), and the short-lived wealth of the wicked (Zophar, chap. 20).[8]

All along, though, Job maintains his innocence, rebukes his "sorry comforters" (16:2) for their insensitivity and pat answers, and pleads for their pity. However, Job also continues to declare that God has wronged him (19:6) and that there is no justice (chap. 21).

The Third Cycle of Speeches (Chaps. 22–31)

Desperately trying to drive home their point of suffering being sin's just reward, Job's counselors now begin to accuse Job of specific sins—among them, spiritual stubbornness and neglect of the needy. Job, however, stands his ground and refutes their assertions. He still longs to plead his case before Almighty God, though he maintains

---

7. Mason, The Gospel According to Job, p. 131.

8. Roy B. Zuck, "Job," in The Bible Knowledge Commentary, Old Testament edition, ed. John F. Walvoord and Roy B. Zuck (Wheaton, Ill.: Scripture Press Publications, Victor Books, 1985), p. 736.

that God has denied him justice (27:2).

Job, still unconsoled by his friends, continues his lament:

> "Oh that I were as in months gone by,
> As in the days when God watched over me;
> When His lamp shone over my head,
> And by His light I walked through darkness."
> (29:2–3)

In a final attempt to show that his suffering is unjustified, Job reflects on the blessing, position, and respected ministry he enjoyed before his affliction (chaps. 29, 31). But now he has become a freak of society, enduring public humiliation and intense physical and emotional pain (chap. 30). "Show me where I have sinned," Job demands in chapter 31, "and I will accept my lot."

At the end of chapter 31, the heated debate between Job and his three friends comes to an end. Job will not speak again until chapter 40. For eight chapters he will listen—first, to another human counselor; then, to God Himself.

Correction in Job's Suffering (Chaps. 32–41)

Elihu

A fourth individual, Elihu, has sat silently and listened to the ongoing debate. A young man, Elihu has respectfully given the older men a chance to speak first (32:4). But he can contain himself no longer. Not only does Elihu see the counsel of the other three men as of no value to Job (v. 3), he thinks Job has come across as self-righteous in his defense (v. 2). He sides with neither Job nor Job's accusers; he goes after them all.

Though direct and sometimes brash, Elihu is less condemning than the others. He seems to have some sympathy for Job's predicament and is the first to suggest suffering as divine discipline rather than judgment for sin (chaps. 32–37).

Job remains silent after Elihu's speech. Maybe this young man's words caused Job to think more deeply about God and His sovereign purposes for suffering—priming the pump for a visit from God Himself.

God

Who knows why God waits until chapter 38 to speak? Perhaps He wanted Job to exhaust all the human arguments for suffering first. Or maybe by appearing to Job in his lowest moment, God shows Himself all the more sufficient. Whatever the reason, God now has the floor. And, ironically, God speaks fewer words than Job or any of his friends.

Interestingly, God doesn't give Job the kind of hearing he wants; He doesn't explain Himself. Rather, He asks Job a list of questions he cannot answer: "Where were you when I laid the foundation of the earth!" (38:4). "Do you know the ordinances of the heavens, Or fix their rule over the earth?" (38:33). "Do you know the time the mountain goats give birth?" (39:1).

God's words turn the eyes of Job's heart from his personal suffering to God's perfect sovereignty (40:3–5).

Submission under Suffering (42:1–6)

Reeling from a personal visit with Almighty God, Job repents for having questioned God's motives and integrity. Though Job never receives an explanation for his suffering, he realizes at last that God is not his enemy, but his friend.

Knowing who God is seems to be enough for Job. And so it must be for us sometimes. God's perspective and His purposes are so much higher than ours, we can trust that He understands our suffering even when we don't. And we can trust that He is Lord over all—even adversity.

Restoration from Suffering (42:7–17)

After Job's confession, God rebukes Eliphaz, Bildad, and Zophar for presenting Job with a distorted picture of God. Elihu isn't mentioned, perhaps because, though he also missed the mark, he came closer than the others to blending sound theology with sincere compassion. God graciously accepts Job's sacrifice as appeasement for His wrath against the three counselors.

Finally, God restores Job to a greater state of blessing and prosperity than he had known before, even giving him ten more children. And after a full life, "Job died, an old man and full of days" (42:17). That phrase, Mike Mason tells us, is "a Biblical expression signifying not merely longevity but fullness of wisdom and godliness."[9]

9. Mason, *The Gospel According to Job*, p. 445.

Job ended as he had begun, blameless and upright, yet with a polished glow that only the abrasive rub of suffering could bring. When it was time to go, he entered into the presence of the Lord, experiencing the full meaning of what he had uttered earlier in his life:

"And as for me, I know that my Redeemer lives,
And at the last He will take His stand on the earth.
Even after my skin is destroyed,
Yet from my flesh I shall see God." (19:25–26)

Living Insights

Suffering is unspiritual.

That's what prosperity theologians, "possibility thinkers," and Job's friends would have us believe. Our suffering certainly doesn't indicate any shortcoming in God. So, there must be something wrong with us. We're harboring unconfessed sin. We're not praying enough. We don't have enough faith. We're not giving enough. That's why we're not healthy, wealthy, and wise.

While it's true that our own sinful choices can bring suffering—sexual promiscuity, for example, can result in AIDS—not all suffering is a direct result of personal sin. How do we know that? Because Jesus suffered immensely, and He never sinned.

No, suffering is part of God's plan to develop our faith, not destroy it. That's what the Cross of Christ is all about. The road to exaltation goes through humility. We gain life by losing it. We know God's strength through our weakness. We get to Easter Sunday through Good Friday. We reach the throne through the Cross.

So be encouraged. The next hardship you face may be a sign that you're growing, not backsliding. That God is for you, not against you. That you are His intimate friend, not His hated enemy. That He is embracing you, not abandoning you.

Nobody likes sitting on ash heaps. But sometimes sitting atop a high ash heap is the best way to get a glimpse into heaven.

Chapter 5

PSALMS: INSPIRED ANTHOLOGY OF PRAISE

A Survey of Psalms

Emerging from the valley of Job's pain, we now face the breath-taking mountain range of the Psalms. With its peaks of praise, clefts of comfort, trails of tears, and green meadows of gratitude, the Psalms, above all, offer us vistas of trust in our almighty God.

Everywhere we turn, we see the myriad facets of our relationship with God refracted through the prism of poetry. Not an elitist poetry that proudly defies anyone to make sense of it, but honest words that open the heart before a loving God. Saint Augustine called the Psalms the "language of devotion";[1] and here we learn to devote ourselves to the One who is devoted to us.

The Psalms are borne out of people's experience. They are devotional; all the climates of the heart, soul, and mind are brought before the unfailing love of God. They are theology, not as it is learned, but as it is lived. The Psalms

teach us about life and God
express pain and desperation
ask for God's mercy and help
nestle us in the Lord's comfort
describe God's character
show us how to approach God
remind us of God's majesty
affirm God's care for us
proclaim God's glory
reflect on the meaning of History
extol God's righteous Law
cry for good to triumph over evil
prophesy God's future justice
show us what is praiseworthy
teach us gratitude
encourage care for the poor and needy
foster trust in the God who wants to bless us

1. Saint Augustine, as quoted by A. F. Kirkpatrick, in *The Book of Psalms*, Thornapple Commentaries series (1902; reprint, Grand Rapids, Mich.: Baker Book House, 1982), p. cv.

PSALMS

	Book One 41 Psalms	Book Two 31 Psalms	Book Three 17 Psalms	Book Four 17 Psalms	Book Five 44 Psalms
	HUMANITY	DELIVERANCE	SANCTUARY	REIGN OF GOD	WORD OF GOD
	PSALMS 1–41	PSALMS 42–72	PSALMS 73–89	PSALMS 90–106	PSALMS 107–150
Analogy	Genesis	Exodus	Leviticus	Numbers	Deuteronomy
Content	Personal	Devotional	Liturgical, Historical	General	Prophetical, Natural
Doxology	Psalm 41:13	Psalm 72:18–19	Psalm 89:52	Psalm 106:48	Psalm 150
Christ in Psalms	Jesus Christ is anticipated, portrayed, and prophesied in such images as the coming King, the Redeemer, the loving Shepherd and the Righteous Sufferer.				

Truly, as Martin Luther said, the Psalms are "a Bible in miniature."[2]

Let's open this book, then, surveying its contents and drawing out some of its beauty and meaning.

Background

Knowing a little of the background of this book will help us grasp its shape and purpose.

Title

The name *Psalms* comes from the Greek word *psalmos* (plural *psalmoi*). It means "poems sung to the accompaniment of stringed instruments." The Greek Septuagint assigned the name to this collection of devotional poems, and the Latin Vulgate followed suit. In Hebrew, the book of Psalms was originally called *Tehillim*, meaning "praises," and sometimes *Tephillot*, which means "prayers."[3]

These names give us a clue to the Psalms' original use. Some were used as part of temple liturgy in both Solomon's temple and the rebuilt temple, making them a Hebrew hymnal for worship and celebration of Feast days and Sabbaths. Others were used for the nation's individual and family devotional life.

Time Frame and Authorship

The Psalms represent a vast collection of spiritual poetry spanning nearly a thousand years. Probably the earliest author is a weary, wandering Moses, who composed Psalm 90.

> Relent, O Lord! How long will it be?
> Have compassion on your servants. . . .
> Make us glad for as many days as you have afflicted
> us,
> for as many years as we have seen trouble.
> (vv. 13, 15)[4]

2. Martin Luther, as quoted by Kirkpatrick in *The Book of Psalms,* p. cvi.

3. J. Sidlow Baxter, *Explore the Book,* six vols. in one (Grand Rapids, Mich.: Zondervan Publishing House, Academie Books, 1966), vol. 3, pp. 84–85; John H. Stek, introduction to Psalms, in *The NIV Study Bible,* ed. Kenneth L. Barker and others (Grand Rapids, Mich.: Zondervan Bible Publishers, 1985), p. 781.

4. In this chapter, we are using the New International Version rather than the New American Standard Bible because we feel that in many instances it conveys the emotion and imagery a little more clearly.

Almost half of the psalms, seventy-three of them, are ascribed to David. Acts 4:25–26 also credits him with Psalm 2, and Hebrews 4:7 tells us he wrote Psalm 95. Solomon wrote two psalms (Ps. 72; 127). Twelve are ascribed to Asaph (Ps. 50; 73–83), which would include those psalms penned by the Asaph who was David's contemporary as well as Asaph's descendants who wrote about the Babylonian exile (Ps. 74; 79). One apiece came from Heman (Ps. 88) and Ethan (Ps. 89) the Ezrahites. Asaph, Heman, and Ethan were Levite singers, musicians, and prophets who served in the tabernacle worship during David's time (see 1 Chron. 15:19; 16:7; 25:5; 2 Chron. 5:12; 29:30).

Eleven psalms come from the sons of Korah (Ps. 42; 44–49; 84–85; 87–88), whose lineage speaks of God's holy wrath as well as His mercy. Korah, a descendant of Levi, along with Dathan and Abiram, led a rebellion against his cousins Moses and Aaron (Num. 16). The three rebels were destroyed by the Lord when the earth split open and "swallowed them, with their households and all Korah's men and all their possessions" (vv. 31–32). Korah's line, however, did not die out (26:11), but they served as gatekeepers of the tabernacle and both temples, as well as ministering as sacred singers (1 Chron. 9:19; 26:19).

Finally, about fifty of the psalms are anonymous, though tradition attributes some of them to Ezra.[5]

The psalms range, then, from the time of the Exodus to after the Exile.

Poetic Form

Hebrew poetry, as we have seen, does not rhyme. Rather, one line parallels the next, either by repeating the same idea in other words, by setting up a contrast, or by completing and expanding on the thought. C. S. Lewis found this poetic form providential.

> Parallelism . . . is (according to one's point of view) either a wonderful piece of luck or a wise provision of God's, that poetry which was to be turned into all languages should have as its chief formal characteristic one that does not disappear (as mere metre does) in translation.[6]

5. Bruce Wilkinson and Kenneth Boa, *Talk Thru the Old Testament*, vol. 1 of *Talk Thru the Bible* (Nashville, Tenn.: Thomas Nelson Publishers, 1983), p. 152.

6. C. S. Lewis, *Reflections on the Psalms* (New York, N.Y.: Harcourt Brace Jovanovich, 1958), pp. 4–5.

Superscriptions

One thing to pay close attention to in reading many of the psalms is the line just above the first verse. These lines are called *superscriptions*, and they often tell us who wrote the psalm and under what circumstances. For example, above Psalm 3 we find, "A psalm of David. When he fled from his son Absalom." Or above Psalm 42, "For the director of music. A maskil of the Sons of Korah." Or Psalm 92, "A psalm. A song. For the Sabbath day."

The meanings of many of the descriptions are obscure now. They seem to have been copied down faithfully by compilers who had long lost touch with their original Hebrew meaning but who wanted to preserve what was written anyway. We can speculate on what some of the words mean, though, by trying to ferret out their roots. *Maskil*, for example, is used thirteen times (Ps. 32; 42; 44; 45; 52–55; 74; 78; 88; 89; 142). It "is most likely related to the root *s-k-l* ('be wise,' 'instruct')," suggesting a teaching psalm. "Other suggestions include 'a skillful psalm,' 'a meditation,' and 'harmony.'"[7] *Mikhtam*, used six times (Ps. 16; 56–60), may mean "a golden psalm, a private prayer, epigram, an atonement psalm, inscription."[8]

Many words also appear to be musical instructions: "on stringed instruments"; "for flute accompaniment"; "on Muth-labben"—meaning "to the tune of 'Death to the Son'"; "upon Aijeleth Hashashahar"—meaning "to the tune of 'The Hind of the Morning'"; "according to the Shoshannim"—meaning "to the tune of 'Lilies'"; "For the Choir Director"; and so forth.

Often, these superscriptions help us get a feel for the emotion, purpose, and use of the psalm.

Selah

Another word you'll notice frequently in the Psalms is *Selah*. Though its exact meaning is uncertain now, many commentators believe it could indicate a pause, a crescendo, or a musical interlude. It could very well mean, "Pause, and think on that."

---

7. Willem A. VanGemeren, "Psalms," in *The Expositor's Bible Commentary*, 12 vols., gen. ed. Frank E. Gaebelein (Grand Rapids, Mich.: Zondervan Publishing House, 1991), vol. 5, p. 38.

8. VanGemeren, "Psalms," p. 38.

Overview

Now that we understand some of the book's background, let's look at the Psalter itself.

Structure

The book of Psalms is divided into five collections:

Book 1: Psalms 1–41
Book 2: Psalms 42–72
Book 3: Psalms 73–89
Book 4: Psalms 90–106
Book 5: Psalms 107–150

Commentator Franz Delitzsch noted an important connection regarding this structure: "The Psalter is also a Pentateuch, the echo of the Mosaic Pentateuch, from the heart of Israel. It is the fivefold book of the congregation to Jehovah, as the Law is the fivefold book of Jehovah to the congregation."[9]

J. Sidlow Baxter expands on this idea.

> There are those who have seen an even closer correspondence between the Book of Psalms and the Pentateuch. . . . The first group [of Psalms], corresponding with Genesis, has much to say about *man*. The second group, corresponding with Exodus, has much to say about *deliverance*. The third group, corresponding with Leviticus, has its emphasis in the Asaph psalms, upon the sanctuary. The fourth group, corresponding with Numbers, and beginning with Psalm [90], the prayer of Moses, stresses the time when unrest and wandering will cease in the coming worldwide kingdom when the nations shall bow to God's King. The fifth group, corresponding with Deuteronomy, has much of thanksgiving for the Divine faithfulness, and lays much emphasis upon the word of the Lord, as, for instance, in the longest of all the psalms, which has for its theme the written word of the Lord [Ps. 119]. We suggest to the student that here, at least, is a very interesting field for exploration.[10]

9. Franz Delitzsch, as quoted by Baxter in *Explore the Book,* p. 87.

10. Baxter, *Explore the Book,* p. 87.

Each of the five books within Psalms concludes with a doxology that isn't necessarily part of the last psalm of that section. They all, however, bless the Lord and praise Him with uninhibited delight (see Ps. 41:13; 72:18–19; 89:52; 106:48; and the exultant Ps. 150).

Types

Although praise permeates Psalms, not all of the psalms are about praise. Major themes—including the character of God, the person of the Messiah, and the triumphs and trials of God's people—are expressed in a variety of forms.

Hymns. These are songs of praise to God and were probably part of Israel's community worship (for example, see Ps. 8; 29; 103; 146).

Lament. Lament psalms occur more frequently than any other type, making up nearly a third of the book. They describe a situation of suffering, plea for God's deliverance, praise Him as an expression of confidence, often make a vow stemming from gratitude, and acknowledge guilt or proclaim innocence (for example, see Ps. 7; 12; 17; 55; 57; 142). Sometimes they include a curse hurled at the ones causing the suffering, which is why some are called *imprecatory psalms* (for example, see Ps. 58; 69; 109; 137). The psalmist gives vent to his feelings—but leaves vengeance in God's hands.

Thanksgiving. These psalms exalt God's wonderful works, and though they have a strong element of praise, their main emphasis in on expressing gratitude (for example, see Ps. 100; 118; 136).

Royal. These apply to Israel's kings, but they often point toward the ultimate King as well (for example, see Ps. 20; 21; 72).

Pilgrim. Pilgrim psalms, sometimes called songs of ascents, were used by the Jews when they went up to Jerusalem for their major festivals (for example, see Ps. 120–134).

Wisdom. Addressing righteous living, the problem of evil, the suffering of the righteous, and God's justice, these psalms primarily emphasize listening and learning (for example, see Ps. 1; 15; 37; 49; 73).

Enthronement. These psalms celebrate God's Kingship and are characterized by phrases such as, "The Lord reigns" and "The Lord Most High is . . . a great King" (for example, see Ps. 47; 93; 99).

Messianic. Israel's hunger and hope for a personal Messiah make up one category of psalms, but these desires certainly spill over into the other categories also (for example, see Ps. 2; 22; 110).

Application

We have noted authors and titles, superscriptions and selahs, structure and categories—but we have barely entered into the heart of the Psalms. And the heart, really, is the center of it all. The Psalms are not meant simply to be analyzed, like a sterile experiment, but they are meant to be lived, felt.

As you begin to ascend their heights and traverse their depths, keep in sight these two guideposts.

First, *the Psalms will meet your pressing needs.* Because they transcend the age and situation in which they were written, shining with an underlying reality that knows no time, they have the power to touch and transform us today.

The psalmists experience becomes our experience. We read, "He restores my soul," and we are restored. We read, "Be strong, take heart!" and we are strengthened. We feel God's love as we extol it. The psalmist's trust fosters our trust.

Second, *the Psalms afford profound insight.* The Law has been given, and history has been lived, but the Psalms reflect on the *meaning* of what has happened and been decreed. They reveal God's heart and discover the spirit, not just the letter, of all that has taken place.

As we meditate on God's strength and care and bring to mind His character, we become the kind of people He wants us to be. "By the renewing of your mind," Paul urges us, "be transformed" (Rom. 12:2)! The Psalms transform us with God's transcendent power.

 *Living Insights*

The Psalms can teach us many things—theology, righteous living, the beauty of God's Law, hope in the Messiah. And we would do well to study each of these aspects and many more we could find. However, there is one way we can use the Psalms that encompasses and integrates all of these themes: prayer.

When we open our hearts to God—listening for His thoughts, receiving His presence, and giving Him ours—we are praying. Many times, our prayers consist of "Help!" and "Thanks!" as Eugene Peterson has noted.[11] These are certainly honest words, and they're probably the essence of most of our prayers. But if they are *all* that

---

11. Eugene H. Peterson, *The Message: Psalms* (Colorado Springs, Colo.: NavPress, 1994), p. 5.

we pray, then we are missing something. Our prayers lack depth and scope.

By God's grace, we are transformed by what we pray. But if our words are quick and shallow, we won't be very deeply transformed. Our faith won't be shaped into something rich and strong.

This is where the Psalms can help us. Rather than just reading them, we can *pray* them—searching for God's thoughts, receiving His presence, and giving Him ours.

Consider Psalm 8, for example. What better way to help our wobbly faith than to remind ourselves of God's greatness?

> O Lord, our Lord,
> how majestic is your name in all the earth!
> You have set your glory
> above the heavens. (v. 1)

And when we feel forgotten and vastly unimportant in the scheme of things, we can prayerfully recall how God values us.

> When I consider your heavens,
> the work of your fingers,
> the moon and the stars,
> which you have set in place,
> what is man that you are mindful of him,
> the son of man that you care for him?
> You have made him a little lower than the heavenly
> beings
> and crowned him with glory and honor.
> You made him ruler over the works of your hands;
> you put everything under his feet. (vv. 3–6)

The Psalms give us a language of prayer that can root us in "what is the breadth and length and height and depth" of life in the embrace of God's love (see Eph. 3:18 NASB). So enter into them, slowly and thoughtfully, and let God fashion you into Christ's image through the language He inspired (see 2 Cor. 3:18).

Chapter 6

PROVERBS: RELIABLE COUNSEL FOR RIGHT LIVING

A Survey of Proverbs

How significant that the book of Proverbs should follow the book of Psalms! This order quietly emphasizes that a right relationship with God (Psalms) must be the foundation for right living (Proverbs). It also shows that we are not meant to spend all of our lives inside a sanctuary; we must also live in the office, the field, the classroom, the home. We cannot limit God to church only, but we must welcome and follow Him in all aspects of our lives.

Psalms and Proverbs give us balance: Generally, the Psalms deepen our devotional life with God, while Proverbs equips us to cope with daily life and other people.

As we approach Proverbs, what can we expect to find? Bruce Wilkinson and Kenneth Boa crystallize the book's aim:

> The Book of Proverbs was designed to equip the reader in practical wisdom, discernment, discipline, and discretion. These maxims emphasize the development of skill in all the details of life so that beauty and righteousness will replace foolishness and evil as one walks in dependence upon God.[1]

The Background of the Book

How did we come to have this wonderful book of wisdom? Let's take a look at its origins.

This chapter has been adapted from "Vertical Wisdom for Horizontal Living," in the study guide *Selected Studies from Proverbs*, coauthored by Lee Hough, from the Bible-teaching ministry of Charles R. Swindoll (Anaheim, Calif.: Insight for Living, 1994).

1. Bruce Wilkinson and Kenneth Boa, *Talk Thru the Old Testament*, vol. 1 of *Talk Thru the Bible* (Nashville, Tenn.: Thomas Nelson Publishers, 1983), p. 139.

PROVERBS

	Prologue to Wise Living	Principles for Wise Living	Personification of Wise Living
	"The fear of the Lord is the beginning of knowledge." (1:7)	"The fear of the Lord is the instruction for wisdom, and before honor comes humility." (15:33)	"Charm is deceitful, and beauty is vain; but a woman who fears the Lord, she shall be praised." (31:30)
	CHAPTERS 1–9	*CHAPTERS 10:1–31:9*	*CHAPTER 31:10–31*
Emphasis	Wisdom especially for youth	Wisdom for all	
Framework	Subjects and statements . . .	People and problems . . .	Counseling and correction
Style	A book filled with short statements that declare a profound truth providing wisdom for life		
Christ in Proverbs	Wisdom is incarnate in Christ "in whom are hidden all the treasures of wisdom and knowledge" (1 Cor. 1:24, 30; Col. 2:3)		

Name

The Hebrew title is *Mishle Shelomoh*, meaning "Proverbs of Solomon," keying off of Proverbs 1:1, "The proverbs of Solomon the son of David, king of Israel." Rabbinical writings descriptively named it *Sepher Hokhmah*—"Book of Wisdom." But the Latin translation rendered the name *Liber Proverbiorum*, "Book of Proverbs," which was shortened simply to Proverbs.[2]

Authors

From the first verse, we would naturally assume that Solomon was the sole author of Proverbs. After all, Scripture tells us:

> God gave Solomon wisdom and very great discernment and breadth of mind, like the sand that is on the seashore. . . . he was wiser than all men, . . . and his fame was known in all the surrounding nations. He also spoke 3,000 proverbs, and his songs were 1,005. (1 Kings 4:29, 31–32)

And he, indeed, wrote the bulk of this book, though most of his three thousand sayings have been erased by time. Other authors, however, also contributed to Proverbs: Agur the son of Jakeh (chap. 30) and King Lemuel (chap. 31). Also, Solomon tells us in Ecclesiastes that he "pondered, searched out and arranged many proverbs" (12:9), which could make him the possible compiler of the "words of the wise" in Proverbs 22:17–24:22 and the "sayings of the wise" in 24:23–34.

Nearly three hundred years later, King Hezekiah, Judah's greatest reformer, found more of Solomon's maxims and added them to this collection of wisdom (25:1).

Definition

What exactly is a proverb? The Hebrew root for *proverb, mashal,* gives us a clue. It means "to represent, be like," conveying the idea of comparing the familiar with the unfamiliar to teach a guiding principle. Proverbs, by nature, are brief—the majority in this book are two lines. But these short, observant statements declare profound truths that give wisdom for life.

Also, as you read through Proverbs, keep in mind that these

---

2. Wilkinson and Boa, *Talk Thru the Old Testament*, p. 162.

are principles, not intended to be prophecies or promises. For example, Proverbs 12:21 says, "No harm befalls the righteous, But the wicked are filled with trouble." In general, if we do what is right, live honestly, and obey divine and human laws, we are choosing paths of life and not of harm. However, we can probably all think of examples where the righteous have suffered—Job is one, Christ another—and the wicked are rich, successful, and apparently trouble-free. Just link Proverbs with principles, and you'll be fine.

The Contents of the Book

To get a grasp of this comprehensive book, let's look at it through three lenses: subjects and statements, people and problems, and counseling and correction.

Subjects and Statements

We could call the style of Proverbs "sentence wisdom," for a brief statement contains a complete idea. Each proverb, then, stands on its own, usually not connected to what precedes or follows it.

The capsules of truth presented in Proverbs come mostly in one of three kinds of couplets. Some are *contrastive*, using the word *but*, as in 14:21:

> He who despises his neighbor sins,
> But happy is he who is gracious to the poor.

Most of Solomon's proverbs follow this pattern.

Others are *completive*, sometimes using the words *and* or *so*, as in 11:25:

> The generous man will be prosperous,
> And he who waters will himself be watered.

or with one thought expanding on the first, as in 16:24:

> Pleasant words are a honeycomb,
> Sweet to the soul and healing to the bones.

Still others are *comparative*, using the words *better/than* or *like/so*:

> Better is a little with righteousness
> Than great income with injustice. (16:8)

> Like cold water to a weary soul,
> So is good news from a distant land. (25:25)

As we can see from this sampling, the topics addressed encompass the full range of life. Eugene Peterson lists a few for us.

> Honoring our parents and raising our children, handling our money and conducting our sexual lives, going to work and exercising leadership, using words well and treating friends kindly, eating and drinking healthily, cultivating emotions within ourselves and attitudes toward others that make for peace. Threaded through all these items is the insistence that the way we think of and respond to God is the most practical thing we do.[3]

People and Problems

In addition to couplets, a wide cast of characters helps impart Proverbs' truths. You'll find the simple, the wise, the proud, the humble, the violent, the angry, the rich, the poor, the oppressor, the oppressed. Sluggards, liars, and slanderers are juxtaposed with the diligent, the truthful, the peacemakers. One of the most pronounced contrasts is between the adulterous woman and Lady Wisdom (wisdom is personified as a woman throughout Proverbs), who finds her flesh-and-blood equivalent in the "excellent wife" of chapter 31.

With such a mixture of vices and virtues in life, problems will inevitably erupt. But rather than (1) avoid them, (2) distract ourselves from them, or (3) hopelessly surrender to them, Proverbs' practical wisdom can help us (4) work through them to a healthy resolution.[4]

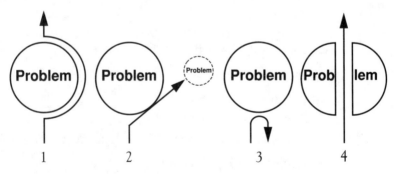

3. Eugene H. Peterson, *The Message: Proverbs* (Colorado Springs, Colo.: NavPress, 1995), p. 3.

4. See Jay E. Adams, *Competent to Counsel* (Phillipsburg, N.J.: Presbyterian and Reformed Publishing Co., 1970), pp. 129–30.

Counseling and Correction

How does Proverbs go about imparting wisdom? In the first section of the book, chapters 1–9, the counsel comes not in couplets but in scenes of wisdom contrasted with folly. These exhortations are still in poetic form, but the thoughts develop through longer discourses. Chapter 10 begins the use of the contrastive, completive, and comparative couplets that run through the middle of chapter 22. In chapters 22 through 24, after a prologue in 22:17–21, many of the proverbs take two verses to complete instead of one. Solomon's couplets resume in chapters 25–29. Then, in chapter 30, Agur introduces numerical proverbs:

> Two things I ask of Thee, . . . (v. 7)

> There are three things that will not be satisfied,
> Four that will not say, "Enough". . . (v. 15b)

> There are three things which are too wonderful
>   for me,
> Four which I do not understand: . . . (v. 18; see
> also vv. 21, 24, 29)

Finally, in chapter 31, King Lemuel shares the wisdom he learned from his mother. He first warns about kings and strong drink (vv. 2–9). Then, in an acrostic poem where each verse begins with a letter of the Hebrew alphabet, he extols the "excellent wife" (vv. 10–31).

So wisdom is presented in many forms: direct commands, observations about life, bad examples, and appealing displays of its many benefits.

The Purposes of the Book

Chapter 1 sets forth five specific purposes of Proverbs. First: *To give reverence to the heart.* Verse 2a says, "To know wisdom and instruction." The term *wisdom* is foundational to this book, so let's understand what it means. Commentator Sid Buzzell explains, "In the Bible's Wisdom literature being wise means being skilled in godly living. Having God's wisdom means having the ability to cope with life in a God-honoring way."[5] Closely connected to wisdom is

5. Sid S. Buzzell, "Proverbs," in *The Bible Knowledge Commentary*, Old Testament edition, ed. John F. Walvoord and Roy B. Zuck (Wheaton, Ill.: Scripture Press Publications, Victor Books, 1985), p. 902.

our need for instruction, which, more than just the communication of facts, means "discipline, chastening, or correction." Taking wisdom and instruction together, then, means humbly receiving God's correction—taking Him seriously—as we sincerely live to honor Him.

Second: *To provide discernment to the eye.* "To discern the sayings of understanding" is the second purpose from verse 2. The word *discern* means "understand, consider, perceive."[6] It's the ability to read between the lines, to distinguish truth from error, right from wrong, good from evil, and be aware of consequences. It's an ethical insight that has as much to do with the mind as it is does the character. And to acquire it, we must be diligent in pursuing it.

Third: *To develop alertness in the walk.* Verse 3 tells us the next purpose, "To receive instruction in wise behavior, Righteousness, justice and equity." These are the ways to "walk in a manner worthy of the God who calls you into His own kingdom and glory" (1 Thess. 2:12). Eugene Peterson elaborates.

> Many people think that what's written in the Bible has mostly to do with getting people into heaven —getting right with God, saving their eternal souls. It does have to do with that, of course, but not *mostly.* It is equally concerned with living on this earth—living well, living in robust sanity. In our Scriptures, heaven is not the primary concern, to which earth is a tag-along afterthought. "On earth *as* it is in heaven" is Jesus' prayer.[7]

Fourth: *To establish discretion and purpose in life.* "To give prudence to the naive, to the youth knowledge and discretion" is the fourth purpose (Prov. 1:4). C. H. Toy defines *discretion* as "the power of forming plans."[8] No longer aimless, the young and the gullible will gain foresight in directing their lives.

Fifth: *To cultivate keenness of mind.* Verses 5–6 reveal the last purpose:

A wise man will hear and increase in learning,

6. R. Laird Harris, Gleason L. Archer, and Bruce K. Waltke, eds., *Theological Wordbook of the Old Testament* (Chicago, Ill.: Moody Press, 1980), vol. 1, p. 103.

7. Peterson, *The Message: Proverbs,* p. 3.

8. C. H. Toy, as quoted by Derek Kidner in *The Proverbs: An Introduction and Commentary* (Downers Grove, Ill.: InterVarsity Press, 1964), p. 37.

And a man of understanding will acquire wise
  counsel,
To understand a proverb and a figure,
The words of the wise and their riddles.

Pondering and probing the *whys* behind the truths presented in Proverbs will stretch any willing mind, broadening and deepening our understanding and our faith.

The Goal of the Book

In closing, notice three key sources of wisdom mentioned in Proverbs 1:7–9:

The fear of the Lord is the beginning of knowl-
  edge;
Fools despise wisdom and instruction.
Hear, my son, your father's instruction,
And do not forsake your mother's teaching;
Indeed, they are a graceful wreath to your head,
And ornaments about your neck.

The fear of the Lord, a father's instruction, and a mother's teaching—all three impart wisdom. And wisdom is not a burdensome load that will weigh down your life but a treasure that will add grace and beauty to your days.

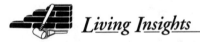 *Living Insights*

How does wisdom differ from common sense? What would a person endowed with good common sense gain from studying Proverbs? Let's take a few minutes to explore this idea.

Common sense tells us to bring an umbrella when the clouds are black and heavy; wisdom tells us that when an emotional storm is brewing, "A gentle answer turns away wrath" (15:1).

Which handles the immediate concern?

_____

Which has more long-range benefits? Why?

_____

Which seems to apply more to moral and ethical issues? Why?

Common sense is valuable, there's no question about that. It can help keep us from catching colds, running out of gas, spending more than we earn—but it doesn't have a spiritual reason for doing what it does. The fear of the Lord is not at the foundation of common sense, as it is with wisdom (1:7; Ps. 111:10).

Also, common sense can help make life easier, but it can't impart life, as wisdom can.

> My son, let them not depart from your sight;
> Keep sound wisdom and discretion,
> So they will be life to your soul. (Prov. 3:21–22a)

> For the commandment is a lamp, and the teach-
>   ing is light;
> And reproofs for discipline are the way of life.
> (6:23)

> Does not wisdom call,
> And understanding lift up her voice? . . .
> "For he who finds me finds life,
> And obtains favor from the Lord." (8:1, 35)

Common sense is good, but it's not enough. We need life and wisdom. We need the love of and respect for the Lord to form the basis of our choices. So, take and read the Proverbs—and grow in the knowledge of God (2:5).

Chapter 7

ECCLESIASTES: SEARCHING FOR THE MEANING OF LIFE

A Survey of Ecclesiastes

Ernest Hemingway lived a full life, or so it seemed.

By age nineteen, he was decorated for heroism in World War I. His first novel, *The Sun Also Rises,* was published when he was only twenty-seven. Hemingway's lifetime itinerary looks like that of a diplomat—the United States, Spain, France, China, Cuba. As a war correspondent during World War II, he was known not only for his writing ability but also for his courage in battle.

He won both the Pulitzer Prize and the Nobel Prize. His virile, gutsy style of writing reflected the way he lived—with gusto. As a big-game hunter, deep-sea fisherman, and bullfighting enthusiast, Hemingway experienced enough danger and adventure for several lifetimes.

But despite such a full life, the novelist was, in fact, unfulfilled. He drank heavily. He married four times. And after a long bout with depression, he took his own life in 1961.[1]

Ernest Hemingway guzzled down all this world had to offer. But in the end, it wasn't enough.

Why not? Why is "the good life" never as good as it seems? And why, after we clean our plates of all the goodies the world serves up, are we still hungry? Why do activity, accomplishment, and pleasure so often fail to fill our famished souls?

Centuries before Hemingway was born, another writer—one who "had it all"—wrestled with those same questions. His reflections, and his instructions for true satisfaction, are recorded for us in the book of Ecclesiastes. So let us feast on his words, and be filled.

Title and Author

The title of the book comes from the writer's identification of himself as "the Preacher" (Eccles. 1:1). The Hebrew word, *Qoheleth,* means "one who addresses an assembly." The Septuagint's title, *Ekklesiastes,* echoed that meaning and eventually yielded our English title, Ecclesiastes.

---

1. *The New Encyclopedia Brittanica,* 15th ed., see "Hemingway, Ernest."

ECCLESIASTES

	Introduction	Investigation and Discoveries	Admonition	Conclusion
	Writer Theme Questions and illustrations	*"I set my mind to seek and explore by wisdom . . ."* PERSONAL PURSUITS Knowledge Amusements Possessions Madness and Folly Labor Philosophy Riches V A N I T Y CONCLUSIONS **Without God's help:** Humans cannot discover what is good for them to do. **Without God's revelation:** Humans do not know what will come after them.	A warning to the young A picture of old age A final admission	THE END OF THE SEARCH Fear God! Obey Him! Someday you will face Him!
	CHAPTER 1:1–11	CHAPTERS 1:12–6:12	CHAPTERS 7:1–11:6	CHAPTERS 11:7–12:8	CHAPTER 12:9–14

Search	Nature	Philosophy	Materialism	Fatalism	Relationships	Theology
Style	Proverbial			Personal		Poetical
Key Verses			2:11; 12:13–14			
Main Theme		The meaninglessness of life apart from God				
Christ in Ecclesiastes		The "One Shepherd" (12:11) who offers abundant life				

60

Although no specific names or dates appear in the book, evidence suggests that Solomon was its author. The writer identifies himself as a son of David and as a king (1:1, 12). He also speaks of his vast wisdom (v. 16), pursuit of pleasure (2:1–3), accomplishments (vv. 4–6), and wealth (vv. 7–10). Solomon certainly would have fit these descriptions.

Some have interpreted Solomon's writing as the product of a midlife crisis. It's probable, though, that Solomon wrote Ecclesiastes toward the end of his life as he reflected on all his accomplishments and failures.

Subject Matter

Ecclesiastes deals with the futility of trying to live and enjoy life apart from God.

> The word *vanity* appears thirty-seven times to express the many things that cannot be understood about life. All earthly goals and ambitions when pursued as ends in themselves lead to dissatisfaction and frustration. Life "under the sun" (used twenty-nine times) seems to be filled with inequities, uncertainties, changes in fortune, and violations of justice.[2]

This focus has led some to interpret Ecclesiastes as pessimistic or skeptical, even heretical. But such is not the case. The book also

> develops the positive theme of overcoming the vanities of life by fearing a God who is good, just, and sovereign.[3]

The book in some ways parallels the book of Job. Where Job emphasizes God's sovereignty in suffering that seems senseless, Ecclesiastes shows His purpose in a life that seems meaningless.

Literary Style

Ecclesiastes—like Job, Psalms, Proverbs, and Song of Solomon—falls into the categories of poetry and wisdom literature. It artfully and emotionally instructs us on how to shine the eternal light of heaven into daily life on earth.

2. Bruce Wilkinson and Kenneth Boa, *Talk Thru the Old Testament*, vol. 1 of *Talk Thru the Bible* (Nashville, Tenn.: Thomas Nelson Publishers, 1983), p. 170.

3. Wilkinson and Boa, *Talk Thru the Old Testament*, p. 170.

Structure

Other than the recurrence of *vanity* (a word that also frames the book: 1:2; 12:8) and the concept of "life under the sun," there is no clear-cut or universally agreed upon structure to Ecclesiastes.

We recommend looking at the book as a four-part discourse from the Preacher: introduction (1:1–11), investigations and discoveries (1:12–11:6), admonition (11:7–12:8), and conclusion (12:9–14).

Introduction (1:1–11)

After introducing himself in the first verse, the Preacher gets right to his topic:

> "Vanity of vanities," says the Preacher,
> "Vanity of vanities! All is vanity." (1:2)

The Hebrew word for *vanity* refers to that which is "without real substance, value, permanence, significance, or meaning."[4] What things qualify as "vanity"? All things "under the sun" (v. 9), which the greater context of the book reveals as all human endeavors performed independently of God.

Solomon supports his thesis with illustrations from the seemingly endless and meaningless cycles found in history and nature. By connecting humanity's work (v. 3) with the rising and setting sun, the capricious wind, and the constantly flowing rivers, Solomon suggests that we are locked into an endless cycle of activity that has no lasting significance. Things go on as they always have and as they always will.

> That which has been is that which will be,
> And that which has been done is that which will
> be done.
> So, there is nothing new under the sun. (v. 9)

Investigation and Discoveries (1:12–11:6)

In the largest section of the book, the Preacher provides more illustrations of futility, this time from his own experience as "king

---

4. Donald R. Glenn, "Ecclesiastes," in *The Bible Knowledge Commentary*, Old Testament edition, ed. John F. Walvoord and Roy B. Zuck (Wheaton, Ill.: Scripture Press Publications, Victor Books, 1985), p. 979.

over Israel in Jerusalem" (v. 12). "You want to see vanity?" he asks implicitly. "Take a look at my life."

Personal Pursuits (1:12–6:12)

The Preacher examines his list of personal resources and, one by one, pronounces all his possessions, passions, and projects to be "vanity and striving after the wind" (v. 14).

He begins by focusing on the hollowness of human achievement in general. All human activities—everything "that has been done under heaven" (v. 13) and "under the sun" (v. 14)—are burdensome and meaningless. Not even the great wisdom Solomon possessed could satisfy him. Rather, his growing awareness and understanding brought increasing grief and pain (v. 18).

How can that be? How could the man upon whom God lavished such wisdom assess that gift as valueless? Perhaps he's speaking here of mere human understanding, apart from God. Or perhaps he's referring to godly wisdom that heightened his own awareness of sin, thus bringing grief and pain.

The Preacher also tried to find meaning in the pursuit of pleasure. He filled his life with laughter, wine, work, women, building, beauty, and riches. Yet again he found all these "vanity and striving after wind and there was no profit under the sun" (2:11).

Though wisdom is superior to foolishness, argues the Preacher, death comes to both the wise and the foolish, so insight and senselessness are meaningless (v. 16). Labor also does not produce any lasting value, since someone foolish can come along after you die and mishandle what you left behind (vv. 18–23).

To our relief, a shaft of light finally breaks into Solomon's dismal reflection, as he suggests that we can truly enjoy life (eat, drink, and labor, vv. 24–26) if we see them as good gifts from the hand of God.

Everything in life—birth, death, weeping, laughter—comes to pass in its own time, and our existence doesn't change that fact (3:1–11). The pulse of earthly activity seems meaningless, unless we see it as part of God's sovereign supervision. Just as Job discovered that there is a good God behind seemingly senseless suffering, Solomon discovered that there is a purposeful God behind the seemingly meaningless flow of life (vv. 12–14).

There is also a time for judgment. God will judge both the wicked and the righteous according to their deeds (vv. 16–17). And as all people must face God, so they must all face death, the great equalizer (vv. 18–21). Therefore, we should enjoy life while we have it (v. 22).

In chapter 4, the Preacher begins to examine the whole range of social relationships. Oppression, competition, isolation, and advancement—all are "vanity and striving after the wind" (4:16). Even our relationship with God is meaningless if it is limited to lip service and thoughtless religion (5:1–7).

Government doesn't provide life's ultimate meaning either, for it is a breeding ground for corruption (vv. 8–9). And wealth also fails to fulfill. If we fall in love with money, we will never have enough, and we'll worry about our possessions. True joy comes when we see riches, and all of life, as a gift from God to be enjoyed (vv. 10–20). Otherwise, everything we accomplish and accumulate during life is meaningless (6:1–12).

Conclusions (7:1–11:6)

In light of all Solomon has experienced, he concludes that the way of wisdom is the path to a full life. He gives lessons in practical wisdom in 7:1–9:12; then he contrasts wisdom with folly in 9:13–11:6. Authors Wilkinson and Boa summarize the writer's presentation of wisdom this way:

> [The writer] portrays levity and pleasure-seeking as superficial and foolish; it is better to have sober depth of thought. Wisdom and self-control provide perspective and strength in coping with life. One should enjoy prosperity, and consider in adversity that God made both. Avoid the twin extremes of self-righteousness and immorality. Sin invades all men, and wisdom is cut short by evil and death. The human mind cannot grasp ultimate meaning. Submission to authority helps one avoid unnecessary hardship, but real justice is often lacking on earth. The uncertainties of life and certainty of the grave show that God's purposes and ways often cannot be grasped. One should, therefore, magnify opportunities while they last, because fortune can change suddenly.[5]

Wisdom is better than the way of fools, says Solomon, for folly brings personal humiliation, grief, and misfortune. Each day is an opportunity to live in wisdom rather than folly.

---

5. Wilkinson and Boa, *Talk Thru the Old Testament*, p. 173.

Admonition (11:7–12:8)

Seeing life as an opportunity to live wisely or foolishly, the Preacher exhorts youth to enjoy life as a gift from God while they are young (11:7–12:1). Old age can be a dark and dismal time (12:2–8), so the sooner we learn to walk with God and enjoy Him, the better.

Conclusion (12:9–14)

If we overlook these final few verses of the book, we will miss both the source and substance of Solomon's message. His reflections have not been the empty musings of earthly wisdom. Rather, the author's words come from the heart of the "Shepherd" (v. 11). Walter C. Kaiser Jr. explains that Solomon's recognition of a heavenly author keeps us from seeing Ecclesiastes as cynical rambling.

> This can only mean Jehovah (or, more accurately, Yahweh), the Shepherd of Israel (Psalm 80:1). He is the real source of the words of this book; not cynicism, not skepticism, not worldliness—not any of these sources. He gave the ideas and aided Solomon in the composition of Ecclesiastes.[6]

And the main substance of Solomon's message?

> Fear God and keep His commandments, because this applies to every person. For God will bring every act to judgment, everything which is hidden, whether it is good or evil. (12:13–14)

After reflecting on the ebb and flow of all life, including his own, Solomon concludes that God is our purpose. He is our meaning. He is the only goal worth pursuing. If we walk with Him, we not only enjoy life, but we prepare ourselves for eternal life.

It's not life "under the sun," then, that brings true meaning, purpose, and joy; but life "under the Son." The best life is a godly life.

Living Insights

"What is the chief end of man?" begins the shorter Westminster Catechism. The answer? "Man's chief end is to glorify God, and to

---

6. Walter C. Kaiser Jr., *Quality Living* (Chicago, Ill.: Moody Press, 1979), p. 156.

enjoy him forever."[7]

The theologians who convened at Westminster to hammer out a summary of the Bible's contents brought together two aspects of the Christian life that we often keep poles apart: piety and pleasure. Too often, we assume that real godliness must come at the expense of enjoyment, or that we can't experience true joy and fulfillment as long as God's in the picture. In other words, we have only two choices: a life we deplore but God loves, or a life we love but God deplores.

Both the catechism and Ecclesiastes, however, remind us that the Christian life was never meant to be dull servitude to a God who's a drag to be with. Sure, the Christian life is challenging and often painful. But as we walk with Christ, we can experience purpose and joy in even the most mundane and painful moments of life.

How about you? Are you glorifying God *and* enjoying Him? Does pleasing Him—obeying His Word, worshiping Him, loving His people—also please you? Or are you looking outside your walk with God for real enjoyment? How would you summarize your walk with God at this point in your life?

_____

_____

_____

_____

_____

Do you need a reminder that the Christian life is the good life or that walking with God is the path to joy? Perhaps it's time to revisit the Psalms. Here are just a few that speak of delight in the Lord:

Psalm 16:11	Psalm 23
Psalm 19:7–11	Psalm 34:8–10
Psalm 21:1–6	Psalm 37:1–6

Enjoy.

7. *The Westminster Standards* (Philadelphia, Pa.: Great Commission Publications, n.d.), p. 71.

Chapter 8

SONG OF SOLOMON: POEM OF FAITHFUL LOVE

A Survey of Song of Solomon

After the disturbing reflections of Ecclesiastes, how delightful is the exuberant love poetry of the Song of Solomon! How opposite these two books are: the first is practically silent about love; the second celebrates the greatest of human loves. Eugene Peterson helps us understand the richness hidden in the contrastive coupling of these books.

> The Song-Ecclesiastes polarity sets the ecstatic experience of love in tension with the boredom of the same old round. The life of faith has to do with the glories of discovering far more in life than we ever dreamed of; the life of faith has to do with doggedly putting one flat foot in front of the other, wondering what the point of it all is. Neither cancels out the other; neither takes precedence over the other. As we sing and pray the lyrics of the Song of Songs, we become convinced that God blesses the best that human experience is capable of; as we ponder the sardonic verses of Ecclesiastes, we recognize the limits inherent in all human experience, appreciate it for what it is, but learn not to confuse it with God.
>
> In such ways, these Wisdom writers keep us honest with and attentive to the entire range of human experience that God the Spirit uses to fashion a life of holy salvation in each of us.[1]

"The best that human experience is capable of"—the intimate love of husband and wife. This is Solomon's theme. And this is one of God's greatest gifts to us.

---

1. Eugene H. Peterson, *The Message: The Wisdom Books* (Colorado Springs, Colo.: NavPress, 1996), p. 7.

SONG OF SOLOMON

	The Courtship	The Wedding		The Maturing Marriage		
	CHAPTERS 1:2–3:5	CHAPTERS 3:6–5:1		CHAPTERS 5:2–8:14		
Emphasis	Bride muses about her beloved	Groom speaks tenderly to his bride	Wife longs for and describes her loving husband	Husband speaks of his wife in intimate terms	Both partners declare a permanent seal on their love	
Chief Speaker	The Bride ("Darling")	The Groom ("Beloved")	Wife ("Darling")	Husband ("Beloved")	Duet	
Key Verse			8:7			
Theme		The joy and intimacy of love within the committed marriage relationship				
Christ in Song of Solomon		Foreshadows the bridegroom relationship of Christ with His church				

Background

The Song of Solomon has been called "perhaps the most difficult and mysterious book in the entire Bible."[2] Widely differing interpretations abound, often adding to the confusion rather than clearing it up. So before delving into the Song itself, let's lay a foundation for understanding it by carefully examining some of its background.

Name

The Hebrew name is *Shir Hashirim*, "Song of Songs," which is the name found in the first verse. It means, "The Best Song," similar to the expressions "King of Kings" and "Lord of Lords." Because the first verse attributes this poem to Solomon, it is also called "Song of Solomon."[3]

Author

The opening verse ascribes the book to Solomon: "The Song of Songs, which is Solomon's." Scripture tells us that Solomon not only composed 3,000 proverbs but also 1,005 songs (1 Kings 4:32). He was also gifted with wisdom about plants and animals (v. 33), and his expertise there certainly shows in his Song.

His expertise in love, however, has posed a problem for many people. How could a man who ultimately had seven hundred wives and princesses and three hundred concubines (1 Kings 11:3) possibly be qualified to extol the virtues of monogamous love? Bruce Wilkinson and Kenneth Boa suggest that

> Solomon's relationship with the Shulamite was the only pure romance he ever experienced. The bulk of his marriages were political arrangements. It is significant that the Shulamite was a vineyard keeper of no great means. This book was also written before Solomon plunged into gross immorality and idolatry.[4]

God has indeed placed His treasure in earthen vessels (see 2 Cor. 4:7), but that certainly doesn't diminish His treasure. As

---

2. Jack S. Deere, "Song of Songs," in *The Bible Knowledge Commentary*, Old Testament edition, ed. John F. Walvoord and Roy B. Zuck (Wheaton, Ill.: Scripture Press Publications, Victor Books, 1985), p. 1009.

3. Bruce Wilkinson and Kenneth Boa, *Talk Thru the Old Testament*, vol. 1 of *Talk Thru the Bible* (Nashville, Tenn.: Thomas Nelson Publishers, 1983), p. 177.

4. Wilkinson and Boa, *Talk Thru the Old Testament*, pp. 177–78.

Matthew Henry reminds us, "Let us all learn not to think the worse of good instructions though we have them from those who do not themselves altogether live up to them."[5]

Date

Many commentators believe that, of Solomon's three books in Scripture, his Song was probably the first written, followed by Proverbs, with Ecclesiastes being last. "When a man is young," a rabbi wrote, "he sings songs. When he becomes an adult, he utters practical proverbs. When he becomes old, he voices the vanity of things."[6] Another view has Ecclesiastes coming before Proverbs, reflecting a mid-life crisis, then recovery of mind and spirit.

Interpretations

In an attempt to discover the meaning of the Song of Solomon, scholars have fashioned a variety of interpretive frameworks. The possibilities include (1) *allegory*, which dismisses any literal meaning and believes the Song is a parable of God's love for Israel, Christ's love for His church, or Christ's love for the individual believer. (2) *Type* believes in the literal meaning as well as a greater spiritual meaning that points to our "marriage" relationship with God (see Isa. 54:4–8; 62:5; Eph. 5:22–23). (3) *Drama*, in which three characters perform a primitive play: the maiden, who is faithful to her shepherd lover, spurns wealthy Solomon's advances. (4) *Satire*, which follows the story line of the dramatic view but puts more bite into Solomon's rejection. (5) *Literal* sees the love of two actual people, Solomon and the Shulamite, being celebrated in poetic form.

We will follow the literal method, but the type view is probably the next most probable interpretation.

Language

The language, though explicitly sexual at times, is never crass.

---

5. Matthew Henry, "The Proverbs," in *Commentary on the Whole Bible*, one volume ed. (Grand Rapids, Mich.: Zondervan Publishing House, 1961), p. 734.

6. Midrash Shir Hashirim Rabba 1.1 as quoted by Robert Gordis, *The Song of Songs* (New York, N.Y.: The Jewish Theological Seminary, 1954), p. 56, as quoted by S. Craig Glickman in *A Song for Lovers* (Downers Grove, Ill.: InterVarsity Press, 1976), p. 181. See also Sid S. Buzzell, "Proverbs," in *The Bible Knowledge Commentary*, p. 902; and Matthew Henry, "The Book of Ecclesiastes," in *Commentary on the Whole Bible*, p. 791.

Rather, Solomon uses richly symbolic, highly figurative expressions to create metaphors "which gain much of their meaning from the emotional feelings one associates with them. . . . The emotional associations of the metaphor are a clue to its overall meaning."[7]

So, hair like a flock of goats descending Mount Gilead, teeth like newly shorn ewes, and breasts like fawns are not direct comparisons. Rather, we must key into the thoughts and feelings these images evoke, as well as remember that these expressions reflect an ancient, agrarian culture.

Finally, to follow who is speaking in the NASB, keep in mind that the woman calls the man "beloved," and the man calls the woman "darling." And the "Daughters of Jerusalem" ("Friends" in the NIV) function as a chorus, often providing transitions throughout the Song.

Survey of the Song

We can divide the Song of Solomon into three broad sections: the courtship (1:2–3:5), the wedding (3:6–5:1), and the struggles and growth in marriage (5:2–8:14).

The Courtship (1:2–3:5)

The Song opens with the woman longing for her beloved (vv. 2–4a). His presence is fragrant to her—both in his affection and in his character, which his name represents (v. 3; compare Prov. 22:1). She wants to be near him, brought into "his chambers" (Song of Sol. 1:4a). The Daughters of Jerusalem echo her praise of Solomon, her lover (v. 4b).

Though she loves Solomon, the woman reveals insecurity about her desirability (vv. 5–7). Also, in seeking to be with her beloved, she does not want to appear as a prostitute hanging around the shepherds' camp. She wants to do the right thing the right way.

When Solomon praises his "darling," however, likening her to the choicest of Pharaoh's eye-turning horses and describing how jewels only accent her beauty, the chorus looks on her with favor and offers to make jewelry for her (vv. 9–11).

The woman next tells how intoxicating and unforgettable her lover is, like the most exotic and enticing of perfumes (vv. 12–14).

7. Glickman, A Song for Lovers, pp. 13, 14.

The lover then tells her how beautiful she is (v. 15), and she responds in kind (vv. 16–17).

Chapter 2 shows that she has become a little more secure. Instead of apologizing for her appearance as before, she says, "I am the rose of Sharon, The lily of the valleys" (v. 1). And Solomon affirms her, "Like a lily among the thorns, So is my darling among the maidens" (v. 2). She compliments him in a similar way, then revels in his love for her: "He has brought me to his banquet hall, And his banner over me is love" (v. 4). As her love grows, so does her desire for him (vv. 5–6). She then admonishes the chorus to wait for love until the time is right (v. 7).

In verses 8–14, spring arrives, and with it, the blossoming of their love and longing. Verse 15—"Catch the foxes for us, The little foxes that are ruining the vineyards"—urges diligence in dealing with those things that can harm the relationship. The woman then reiterates her growing security in Solomon's love as well as their mutual, exclusive commitment: "My beloved is mine, and I am his" (v. 16). She finishes by wishing for love's fulfillment when they are finally married (v. 17).

With her love intensifying, the woman experiences anxiety over the fear of losing her lover. This surfaces in a dream, where she searches for the one "whom my soul loves," finds him, and brings him to the safest place she knows—her mother's house (3:1–4). In verse 5, the refrain of waiting repeats (see 2:7). Earlier, desire was not to rush love; now, fear should not rush it either.

The Wedding (3:6–5:1)

Finally, the happy day arrives. In ancient times, as in some cultures still today, the wedding ceremony began with the groom leading a procession to the bride's home. Once the couple were married, a wedding feast would begin that lasted a week or more. The newlyweds, despite the ongoing feast, consummated their marriage on the wedding night. The magnificent procession of Solomon is described in 3:6–11; and his loving words to his "darling" on their wedding night are recorded in chapter 4.

He praises her beauty—her soft, gentle eyes (v. 1a); her shimmering, flowing hair (v. 1b); her inviting, delightful smile (v. 2); her enticing, kissable lips (v. 3a); the blush of her cheeks (v. 3b); her quiet dignity (v. 4); her soft, tender breasts (v. 5). "You are altogether beautiful, my darling," he tells his bride, and his heart and desire are completely hers (vv. 6–11). He also delights in her virginity—"a garden locked is my sister, my bride" (vv. 12–15), and she expresses her desire to be completely his now (v. 16). They consummate their love (5:1a), and God blesses them, "Eat, friends; Drink and imbibe deeply, O lovers" (v. 1b).

The Maturing Marriage (5:2–8:14)

Sometime later, perhaps months after their wedding, the lovers encounter their first problem: the bride's indifference to her husband. In this second of the bride's dreams, she hears her ardent husband's loving overtures but won't bother to get out of bed to let him in (5:2–3). He tries the door, can't open it, then calmly leaves—after putting some myrrh, the equivalent of a love note, on the door handle (vv. 4–5). His tender patience moves the bride's heart, but when she seeks him, she cannot find him (vv. 6–7). Unlike the watchmen in the first dream (3:3), these watchmen strike and hurt her (5:7), probably symbolizing the guilt and pain over this separation.

She turns to the Daughters of Jerusalem for help (v. 8), and when they ask for a description of her beloved (v. 9), she rhapsodizes about how wonderful he is (vv. 10–16). Indifferent no longer, her love and desire for him are fully reawakened. "My beloved is dazzling and ruddy, Outstanding among ten thousand. . . . His mouth is full of sweetness. And he is wholly desirable. This is my beloved and this is my friend, O daughters of Jerusalem" (vv. 10, 16).

Eager to help her find such a man, the Daughters of Jerusalem ask where he might be (6:1). The bride knows where he is physically, and as her heart draws closer toward him, she finds him emotionally: "I am my beloved's and my beloved is mine" (vv. 2–3). Though their relationship will have problems from time to time, she is secure in their commitment to each other. And he reassures her by welcoming her with tender praise, focusing more on loving her than expressing his sexual desire for her to prevent any misunderstanding (vv. 4–9). Happy at their reconciliation, the lovers as well as the Daughters of Jerusalem reiterate their happiness in an antiphony of delight (vv. 10–13).

The lovers' most passionate exchange takes place in chapter 7. Solomon starts at her feet and moves to the top of her head in his praise. He tells his bride how beautiful the curves of her feet, legs and hips are (v. 1), how her body is drink and food for him — satisfying his desires completely (v. 2). Her soft breasts, smooth neck, and warm eyes draw him in, as do the regal features of her face (vv. 4–5a). Her hair especially captivates him (v. 5b). But he is ravished by her breasts and, after making love to her, they fall asleep in each other's arms (vv. 6–9). She basks in the warmth of his desire, "I am my beloved's, And his desire is for me" (v. 10). Then, as a sign of their relationship's growing maturity and freedom, she initiates lovemaking herself, suggesting they get away "into the country . . . There I will give you my love" (vv. 11–13).

As their married love deepens, the bride longs to express her affection publicly, which would only be appropriate in that culture with a family member, such as a brother (8:1). She playfully pretends to lead her lover as an older sister would (v. 2); but then she longs for him to lead in love: "Let his left hand be under my head, And his right hand embrace me" (vv. 2–3). Then, to those who might long for a love like theirs, she says, "Do not arouse or awaken love, Until it pleases" (v. 4 literally).

In these last verses of the Song, we learn of love's nature and power. The Daughters of Jerusalem ask, "Who is this coming up from the wilderness, Leaning on her beloved?" (v. 5a). Out of the wilderness, the couple emerges into the promised land of love. She says that beneath the tree of love, their love was born (8:5b); and, like natural birth, it was not without pain—the pain of longing, insecurity, and separation. She wants to be a seal over his thoughts ("heart") and actions ("arm"), desiring to be his most valued possession (v. 6a).

She states that God created love to be stronger than death—enduring and irreversible (v. 6b). Its "jealousy is as severe as Sheol"—it will not surrender the loved one, just as the Lord burns for His own people and will not give them to another (v. 6c). Love's flame cannot be put out (v. 7a), and no amount of money is enough to buy it (v. 7b). "Love is not only painful, possessive and persevering. It is also priceless. It is priceless because the one who is loved is priceless."[8]

Verses 8–9 tell of her family's concern that she maintain her virginity, which she did, until she married Solomon and gave herself to him (vv. 10–12).

And as their love continues to grow in marriage, he still longs for her (v. 13), and she for him (v. 14).

Would that all of our marriages would reflect the commitment, care, and delight found in the Song of Solomon, the Best of Songs.

8. Glickman, *A Song for Lovers*, p. 101.

 *Living Insights*

What an ideal we have in Solomon's Song for Christian marriages! What freedom to be wildly in love, romantic, tender, and sensual. To be committed, secure, happy.

Then why is it that Christian marriages so often don't look like this? Why are there put-downs, criticisms, alienation, and boredom? Christian friends, what poor lovers we are!

The Song of Songs, by its positive example, can disclose at least four things our marriages need. Think through how you are doing in each area.

1. *The need for personal attention.* Physical love is an art that cannot grow without being nurtured. It requires emotional intimacy, the enjoyment of being with one another, sharing life and love and mutual interests. It depends on knowing and understanding one another deeply. How well do you know your spouse at this point in your marriage? What are his/her dreams, fears, hopes, pleasures, goals?

What communicates love to your partner?

----

2. *The need for leisure.* Creativity, enjoyment, and playfulness only blossom in a relationship when they are cultivated in the soil of time. Have other things crowded out your time with your partner? What are they?

Is being a good lover—in all the senses of that word—a high

priority for you? How much of your time are you willing to devote to this?

_____

_____

3. *The need for meaningful getaways.* Special times away from the clutter and clamor of constant demands can refresh a relationship. When can you take some time to get away? Today, even if it's just to walk hand-in-hand in the park? How about in the next week? How about in the next three months?

_____

_____

_____

_____

4. *The need for security.* Reaching the deepest level of secure, peaceful love takes commitment. Without security, the acid of jealousy can scar a love and ultimately destroy it. What do you need to do to reassure your spouse of your commitment? Restate your wedding vows? Reaffirm your delight in your marriage-lover?

_____

_____

_____

Chapter 9

PROFILE OF A
PROPHET

Selected Scriptures

I remember walking down an Atlanta street with my mother and seeing something quite shocking," writes author A. J. Conyers. "An old man trudged back and forth on the sidewalk. Wild white hair frizzed out from beneath an olive-colored slouch hat. An unkempt beard lapped over a sign hanging from his neck—a sign that said, 'The End Is Near.'"[1]

For many, this frizzed-out fanatic mutely announcing doom on a sandwich board is their image of a prophet. Weird, grim, disconnected from daily reality, knowing something the rest of us don't, and a little smug about it too. But this wild-eyed predictor of future destruction, though similar to God's prophets in his jarring effect, is only a pale—very pale—imitation of the servants God entrusted with His words.

As we stand on the threshold of the Old Testament's prophetical section, let's cast off any false images that may have hindered our desire to enter these books. Let's get to know these prophets—some of the most magnificent people who ever lived—and prepare our hearts for their timeless, penetrating messages.

The Role of the Prophets

The Hebrew Scriptures used three words for those commissioned by God to deliver His prophecies to His people. *Nabi* is the main term, meaning "an announcer or spokesman of God's words."[2] Two other terms, *ro'eh* and *hozeh*, designated a seer—one who saw (a "see-er") in dreams and visions. "The essence of the idea is that God allowed certain people to 'see' (i.e., understand)—or receive

---

1. A. J. Conyers, *The End: What Jesus Really Said about the Last Things* (Downers Grove, Ill.: InterVarsity Press, 1995), p. 13.

2. Gary V. Smith, "Prophet; Prophecy," in *The International Standard Bible Encyclopedia*, revised edition, gen. ed. Geoffrey W. Bromiley (1986; reprint, Grand Rapids, Mich.: William B. Eerdmans Publishing Co., 1987), vol. 3, p. 987.

The Kings and Prophets
The Northern Kingdom: Israel 931–722 B.C.

Prophets	*Kings*	*Godly?*	*Years Reigned*	*Scripture Record*
	Jeroboam I	No	22	1 Kings 12–14
	Nadab	No	2	1 Kings 15
	Baasha	No	24	1 Kings 15–16
	Elah	No	2	1 Kings 16
	Zimri	No	7 days	1 Kings 16
	Omri[3]	No	12	1 Kings 16
Elijah	**Ahab**	No	22	1 Kings 16–22
Elijah	**Ahaziah**	No	2	1 Kings 22; 2 Kings 1
Elijah	**Jehoram (Joram)**	No	12	2 Kings 3–8
Elisha	**Jehu**	No	28	2 Kings 9–10
Elisha	**Jehoahaz (Joahaz)**	No	17	2 Kings 13
Elisha	**Jehoash (Joash)**	No	16	2 Kings 13
Hosea; *Jonah*; *Amos*	**Jeroboam II**	No	41	2 Kings 14
Hosea	**Zechariah**	No	6 months	2 Kings 15
Hosea	**Shallum**	No	1 month	2 Kings 15
Hosea	**Menahem**	No	10	2 Kings 15
Hosea	**Pekahiah**	No	2	2 Kings 15
Hosea	**Pekah**	No	20	2 Kings 15
Hosea	**Hoshea**	No	9	2 Kings 17

Assyrian Captivity: 722 B.C.

The kings of both Israel and Judah are listed in the order of their reigns. Since Scripture refers to some kings by more than one name, alternate names are given in parentheses. The prophets' names appear in boxes to show which prophets ministered under which kings. Not all the prophets are mentioned, only the better known ones.

3. Some commentators consider Tibni, who fought with Omri for the throne, a legitimate king. That would bring the count of Israel's kings to twenty.

* Charts adapted from John F. Walvoord and Roy B. Zuck, eds., *The Bible Knowledge Commentary,* Old Testament edition (Wheaton, Ill.: Scripture Press Publications, Victor Books, 1985), p. 513.

THE KINGS AND PROPHETS
THE SOUTHERN KINGDOM: JUDAH 931–586 B.C.

Kings	Godly?	Years Reigned	Scripture Record
Rehoboam	No	17	1 Kings 12–14; 2 Chron. 11–12
Abijah (Abijam)	No	3	1 Kings 15; 2 Chron. 13
Asa	Yes	41	1 Kings 15; 2 Chron. 14–16
Jehoshaphat	Yes	25	1 Kings 22; 2 Chron. 17–20
Jehoram *Obadiah*	No	8	2 Kings 8; 2 Chron. 21
Ahaziah	No	1	2 Kings 8; 2 Chron. 22
Queen Athaliah	No	6	2 Kings 11; 2 Chron. 22–23
Joash (Jehoash) *Joel*	Yes	40	2 Kings 12–13; 2 Chron. 24
Amaziah	Yes	29	2 Kings 14; 2 Chron. 25
Uzziah (Azariah)	Yes	52	2 Kings 15; 2 Chron. 26
Jotham	Yes	16	2 Kings 15; 2 Chron. 27
Ahaz	No	16	2 Kings 16; 2 Chron. 28; Isa. 7–12
Hezekiah	Yes	29	2 Kings 18–20; 2 Chron. 29–32; Isa. 36–39
Manasseh *Nahum*	No	55	2 Kings 21; 2 Chron. 33
Amon	No	2	2 Kings 21; 2 Chron. 33
Josiah *Zephaniah*	Yes	31	2 Kings 22–23; 2 Chron. 34–35
Jehoahaz (Joahaz)	No	3 months	2 Kings 23; 2 Chron. 36
Jehoiakim *Habakkuk*	No	11	2 Kings 23–24; 2 Chron. 36
Jehoiachin	No	3 months	2 Kings 24; 2 Chron. 36
Zedekiah	No	11	2 Kings 24–25; 2 Chron. 36; Jer. 52

(Vertical prophet markers alongside the table: **Micah** and **Isaiah** span Jotham–Manasseh; **Jeremiah** spans Josiah–Zedekiah.)

BABYLONIAN CAPTIVITY: 586 B.C.

Exilic Prophets: Daniel, Ezekiel, Jeremiah (Lamentations)

Postexilic Prophets: Haggai, Zechariah, Malachi

a divine communication that contained insight into—past, present, or future events."[4]

Prophets were also known by several other descriptive titles: "man of God," "His servant," "His messenger," "watchman." This last name is particularly poignant, describing the prophet as one who would alert the people to coming danger so they would have time to avert it.

This protective role should have been the priests' and Levites'. These men were to teach the people to follow God's laws and stay safely on the path of life. As Moses had said when he blessed the tribe of Levi,

> "They shall teach Thine ordinances to Jacob,
> And Thy law to Israel.
> They shall put incense before Thee,
> And whole burnt offerings on Thine altar."
> (Deut. 33:10)

This consecrated tribe, however, was prone to falling into empty ritualism and even idolatry (just like the rest of Israel), as we saw as early as the book of Judges. Those who were supposed to represent God's holiness to humanity, as well as intercede on the people's behalf, instead corrupted their calling. Israel's and Judah's kings, too, who were supposed to be God's representative rulers, establishing and upholding His righteous and just laws in society, often misused their power and led the nation astray.

So God raised up special messengers who would call the people back to Himself, laying bare their sins and pleading with them to repent and return to their covenant with their Lord.

The Characteristics of True Prophets

Any time God reaches out to save His people, we can be sure that Satan will try to sabotage the rescue by creating a deadly counterfeit. And so he did with prophets. False prophets often rose alongside the true (compare Matt. 13:24–30; 24:11), some lured by money, others by power and status before the king.

How would anyone be able to tell the difference between the false prophets and the true? First, whatever they said had to have

---

4. Smith, "Prophets; Prophecy," p. 987.

come true—without fail (Deut. 18:22). Second, whatever they said must have encouraged passionate obedience to God (13:1–5). And third, nothing they said should have contradicted God's Word, because God never contradicts Himself (Jer. 23:16–22).

True prophets also differed in character from the false. A false prophet would have said anything necessary to keep the king's and people's favor. True prophets, however, spoke the words God told them—no matter how unpopular and opposed they became. Let's take a moment to list some of the character qualities God's prophets showed.

- They were uncompromising individualists, bent on following God's Law and calling sin, sin (see Isa. 1:1–17, 21–23).

- They stood alone against tremendous opposition (see Jer. 1:17–19).

- They were God's mouthpiece (see Jer. 1:4–10).

- They were people of rugged determination (see Ezek. 2:1–7).

- They were people of prayer and communion with God (see Dan. 2:17–23; 6:4–13).

- They displayed remarkable zeal and dedication, obeying God in the most extreme circumstances (see Hos. 1:2–3).

- They were outspoken critics of social evils (see Amos 2:6–8; Hab. 1:1–4).

- They revealed future events (see Mic. 5:2–5; Mal. 3:1).

The Times of the Prophets

To get our bearings on who the prophets were and the times in which they ministered, we can group them in four eras.

United nation: As Jacob's family grew to a nation and then a glorious kingdom, God used a variety of prophets to keep His people on track. Included in this group would be Moses, his sister Miriam, Deborah, Samuel, Nathan, Gad, Zadok, Heman, Asaph, Jeduthun, and Ahijah.

Divided kingdom: When God tore ten tribes away from Rehoboam because of his father, Solomon's, sins, He did not turn His back on His people in either nation. The prophets He sent to the northern kingdom of Israel included Jehu, Elijah, Micaiah, Elisha, Jonah,

Amos, and Hosea. And the prophets who brought God's word to the southern kingdom of Judah included Shemaiah, Iddo, Azariah, Obadiah, Joel, Isaiah, Micah, Nahum, Habakkuk, Zephaniah, and Jeremiah, who witnessed God's people enter captivity.

Exiled people. Because the people did not listen to God's prophets and turn from their faithless and destructive ways, He exiled them from their Promised Land. Israel was conquered and dispersed by the Assyrians in 722 B.C., never to be restored. Judah was taken into captivity by Babylon in three deportations between 605 B.C. and 586 B.C. Though no longer a nation, they were still a people—God's people—and God raised up prophets to encourage and correct them even in a foreign land. These prophets included Jeremiah, who wrote to those in the first two deportations and grieved over the final destruction of Jerusalem in Lamentations, as well as Daniel and Ezekiel.

Restored nation. After the prescribed time of captivity was over, God opened the doors for His people to return to Jerusalem and Judah. To help them resettle the land in His righteousness, He sent Haggai, Zechariah, and Malachi. Once Malachi's words were uttered, four hundred years of prophetic silence ensued until John the Baptizer heralded the coming of the Greatest Prophet, God's Son, Jesus Christ.

The Books of the Prophets

Not all of the prophets wrote down their divine messages. Fortunately, seventeen of them did—five of which we'll be studying in this guide, and the final twelve in the next. The five we'll be looking at here are known as the Major Prophets; the twelve following are called the Minor Prophets. This distinction springs mainly from their size, not their importance. And J. Sidlow Baxter finds another distinguishing factor, saying that the Minor Prophets "do not determine the main shape of Messianic prophecy. They conform to the general frame already formed for us in Isaiah, Jeremiah, Ezekiel and Daniel."[5]

Also, it's helpful to understand the style in which these prophets wrote. The editors of the *New Geneva Study Bible* tell us:

---

5. J. Sidlow Baxter, *Explore the Book*, 6 vols. in one (Grand Rapids, Mich.: Zondervan Publishing House, Academie Books, 1966), vol. 3, p. 200.

A noticeable feature of the prophetic books is that they often bring short passages together whose only connection is that they came from the same prophet. There is little narrative or connective writing, and the original historical reference may be impossible to recover.[6]

So when you read the prophets' messages, follow the natural divisions rather than struggle to connect everything.

The Message of the Prophets

As we have seen, the prophets did a lot more than proclaim, "The end is near." They spoke to their times, rebuking kings, priests, and people for such issues as injustice, corruption, idolatry, empty ritualism, violence, divorce, pride, materialism, greed, and the oppression of the poor and helpless. If they would not heed the rebukes, the prophets warned of God's coming judgment against their faithlessness and sin. If they did repent, however, the prophets assured them of God's mercy, comfort, and blessing. They prophesied judgment and restoration, captivity and return, with startling detail.

They also reminded God's people of God's character—His kindness, His holiness, His mercy, His forgiveness, His love, His sovereignty, His desire to help. The prophets told of the Messiah God would send, the One who would finally free them from their sins and overcome their enemies. And they unveiled the end of time, the awesome Day of the Lord, when sin will be judged and evil finally defeated.

The prophets, then, both foretold the future and forthtold God's word for the present, because the present and the future were closely intertwined. God had long ago set before His people blessings and curses, life and death (Deut. 30:11–20). The prophets strived to make the people aware that the choices they made in their today would shape the future waiting for them in their tomorrow.

Though we don't have prophets today in the biblical sense, the voices of these Old Testament prophets resound with relevant truth. May we have ears that hear, eyes that see, and hearts that will embrace their message.

6. *New Geneva Study Bible*, gen. ed. R. C. Sproul, Old Testament ed. Bruce Waltke (Nashville, Tenn.: Thomas Nelson Publishers, 1995), p. 1018.

 *Living Insights*

As we begin our journey through the prophetic books, how can we delve into them in a more meaningful way than setting dates for the end of the world? Eugene Peterson offers a few words that will help us keep the heart and purpose of prophecy firm in our minds.

> A common way to misunderstand prophecy . . . is to suppose that it means prediction. But that is not the biblical use of the word. Prophets are not fortune tellers. The prophet is the person who declares, "Thus says the Lord." He speaks what God is speaking. He brings God's word into the immediate world of the present, insisting that it be heard here and now. The prophet says that God is speaking now, not yesterday; God is speaking now, not tomorrow. It is not a past word that can be analyzed and then walked away from. It is not a future word that can be fantasized into escapist diversion. . . . The prophetic word eliminates the distance between God's speaking and our hearing. If we make the prophetic word a predictive word we are procrastinating, putting distance between ourselves and the application of the word, putting off dealing with it until some future date. . . . Prophecy points out connections between dailiness and God's eternity and calls us to choose to live these connections.[7]

Yes, the end of time is part of prophecy, there's no dispute about that. But how we live now is deeply a part of the end. A. J. Conyers explains,

> We do not choose the end *at the end*, but we choose our response to the end of things every day that we live. . . .
> . . . The moment in which we live will be remembered at the end of time. It is a component of

7. Eugene H. Peterson, *Reversed Thunder: The Revelation of John and the Praying Imagination* (San Francisco, Calif.: HarperSanFrancisco, 1988), pp. 20–21, 114.

the end. And how we respond to this moment—this poor man in our midst, this starving child in our community, this prisoner in our institutions, the very humblest and meanest of those who enter our lives today—is in fact the way we greet the last moment of life, the last moment of the planet Earth, the first moment of a newly manifest and apparent kingdom of God.[8]

Part of understanding the words of the prophets is understanding the times in which they prophesied. But the greater part of understanding their message is to live it today, because their words—God's words—are not bounded by any time.

8. Conyers, *The End*, p. 53.

Chapter 10

ISAIAH: PRINCE AMONG THE PROPHETS

A Survey of Isaiah

Isaiah.

His eloquent literary style, distinguished Jewish upbringing, and tireless declaration of God's Word have earned him the titles "Prince among Prophets" and "Saint Paul of the Old Testament." Isaiah's contribution, though, lies not in his own princeliness but in his revelation of the Prince of Peace—the Lord Jesus Christ Himself.

As you read Isaiah, you might at times forget that you're in the Old Testament. The book is rich with images of the coming Messiah who would save His people from their sins and eventually establish His holy kingdom on earth. Indeed, Isaiah's listeners needed this message of God's righteousness and His provision of a Savior.

The people of Judah in Isaiah's day were characterized by hypocrisy, greed, self-indulgence, and idolatry. Through Isaiah, God announced His judgments on His covenant-breaking people. He warned that Judah would be invaded and carried into exile by the Babylonian army in the future.

God's message, however, wasn't limited to judgment. He promised that He would redeem His people not only from political oppression but spiritual oppression as well through the coming messianic King. Jesus Christ will usher in the glorious reign of God, creating "new heavens and a new earth" (Isa. 65:17a), where

> "the wolf and the lamb shall graze together, and the lion shall eat straw like the ox; and dust shall be the serpent's food. They shall do no evil or harm in all My holy mountain," says the Lord. (v. 25)

Isaiah: The Man

Judging from Isaiah's artistry with words, he was well educated— very likely born into an aristocratic Jewish family. Herbert Wolf and John Stek provide a fuller description of the prophet.

ISAIAH

	The Judgment of God	The Deliverance of God		
	CHAPTERS 1–39	THE SUPREMACY OF THE LORD CHAPTERS 40–48	THE SERVANT OF THE LORD Servant Songs: 42:1–9 49:1–13 50:4–11 52:13–53:12 CHAPTERS 49–53	THE FUTURE PLAN OF THE LORD CHAPTERS 54–66
Emphasis	The law and judgment for disobedience	God's grace and deliverance Comfort . . . Promise . . . Hope . . .		
"Bible within Bible"	Old Testament	New Testament		
Key Verses	2:3–5; 6:1–3; ch. 53			
Main Theme	The justice and mercy of God			
Christ in Isaiah	His first and second advents are prophesied throughout the book (child of a virgin in 7:14, the shoot from the stem of Jesse in chapter 11, the suffering Servant in chapter 53).			

Isaiah son of Amoz is often thought of as the greatest of the writing prophets. His name means "The Lord saves." He was a contemporary of Amos, Hosea and Micah, beginning his ministry in 740 B.C., the year King Uzziah died. . . . According to an unsubstantiated Jewish tradition (*The Ascension of Isaiah*), he was sawed in half during the reign of Manasseh (cf. Heb 11:37). Isaiah was married and had at least two sons, Shear-Jashub (7:3) and Maher-Shalal-Hash-Baz (8:3). He probably spent most of his life in Jerusalem, enjoying his greatest influence under King Hezekiah (see 37:1–2). Isaiah is also credited with writing a history of the reign of King Uzziah (2 Ch 26:22).[1]

Isaiah's Times

Isaiah ministered for more than fifty years, from 740 B.C. until possibly 686 B.C. or beyond, during the reigns of four kings: Uzziah, Jotham, Ahaz, and Hezekiah. He was a contemporary of three other prophets—Amos and Hosea in the north, and Micah in Judah. This time in the history of the divided kingdom was

a time of great struggle both politically and spiritually. The Northern Kingdom of Israel was deteriorating politically, spiritually, and militarily and finally fell to the Assyrian Empire in 722 B.C. The Southern Kingdom of Judah looked as though it too would collapse and fall to Assyria, but it withstood the attack. In this political struggle and spiritual decline Isaiah rose to deliver a message to the people in Judah. His message was that they should trust in the God who had promised them a glorious kingdom through Moses and David. Isaiah urged the nation not to rely on Egypt or any other foreign power to protect them for the Lord was the only protection they would need.[2]

1. Herbert Wolf and John H. Stek, introduction to Isaiah, in *The NIV Study Bible*, ed. Kenneth L. Barker and others (Grand Rapids, Mich.: Zondervan Bible Publishers, 1985), p. 1014.

2. John A. Martin, "Isaiah," in *The Bible Knowledge Commentary*, Old Testament edition, ed. John F. Walvoord and Roy B. Zuck (Wheaton, Ill.: Scripture Press Publications, Victor Books, 1985), pp. 1029–30.

Though Judah had escaped the Assyrian captivity that befell the northern kingdom of Israel in 722 B.C. (see Isa. 36–37; 2 Kings 17–19), Isaiah foretold that Judah would be plundered in the future (586 B.C.) by Babylon, who would supplant Assyria as the world power (see Isa. 39). But even amid such announcements of coming judgment, Isaiah gave a comforting message of God's loving care and redemption.

Literary Style

Isaiah is a literary work of art. Most of the book was written in vivid, emotional poetry. Chapters 36–39 constitute the main prose section.

Isaiah obviously loved the technique of personification; he used it liberally. The moon and sun are ashamed (24:23), the wilderness and desert are glad (35:1), the mountains and forests shout for joy (44:23), and the trees clap their hands (55:12). His metaphors are also picturesque: Israel is portrayed as a vineyard (5:7), a winepress represents judgment (63:3), and God is a rock of refuge (17:10).

Isaiah is also artfully messianic, showcasing the person and work of Jesus Christ. It's no surprise, then, that

> Isaiah is quoted in the New Testament far more than any other prophet. He is mentioned twenty-one times by name, and chapter 53 alone is quoted or alluded to at least eighty-five times in the New Testament. Isaiah is characterized by systematic presentation, brilliant imagery, broad scope, clarity, beauty, and power.[3]

The Debate about Unity

Some scholars contend that Isaiah could not have written the entire book, saying that at least two people contributed to it. Their conclusions center around historical and linguistic arguments.

The Historical Argument

The historical argument goes something like this: Since chapters 1–39 focus on conditions in Isaiah's day, Isaiah must have written that section. Chapters 40–66, however, depict the period

---

3. Bruce Wilkinson and Kenneth Boa, *Talk Thru the Old Testament*, vol. 1 of *Talk Thru the Bible* (Nashville, Tenn.: Thomas Nelson Publishers, 1983), p. 193.

of Babylonian captivity—which occurred long after Isaiah's death—and the messianic kingdom. That section, then, must have been written by a prophet who lived during the Babylonian exile, a "Deutero-Isaiah" (second Isaiah). Some even suggest that, since chapters 56–66 foretell the second coming of Christ, this section must have been written by a "Tertio" (third) Isaiah, most likely a prophet who lived after the Babylonian exile.

A change in historical perspectives within one book, however, doesn't negate the book's unity. The book of Revelation, for example, mingles past, present, and future, but was written by a single author—the apostle John.

Critics who dispute a single author seem unwilling to believe that God would reveal the future to His prophets. But the sovereign, omnipotent, and omniscient God can do anything. In Isaiah and many of the other prophetic books, He generously shares with us the things to come.

The Linguistic Argument

Critics also argue that variations in language and style indicate multiple authors. The first section is more terse, matching the tone of judgment; while the second section is more flowing, in keeping with the relief of grace and comfort. But all good writers will alter their pace, sentence structure and length, word choice, and phrasing to convey the tone and meaning of their message. Also, similar terms and phrases are repeated throughout the book. Literary images, such as the highway motif, and themes such as the remnant, peace, joy, and judgment appear in both sections.

The New Testament writers certainly considered Isaiah the author of the entire book. Passages throughout Isaiah are quoted in the New Testament—and all are attributed to one writer named Isaiah.

In addition to evidence within the book itself, both Christian and Jewish tradition have long recognized Isaiah as the sole author.

Given these and many other reasons, the multiple author theory is simply unfounded. The book of Isaiah upholds the integrity, beauty, and unity of God's supernatural revelation.

Structural Overview

The overall structure of Isaiah can be easily remembered if we look at the book as a Bible within the Bible. Isaiah has sixty-six chapters, just as the Bible has sixty-six books. Isaiah can be divided into two main sections: chapters 1–39 focus primarily on human sinfulness and the righteousness, holiness, and necessary judgment of God, much like the thirty-nine books of the Old Testament. The next twenty-seven chapters, like the twenty-seven books of the New Testament, stress God's glory, compassion, and redemptive grace as evidenced in the Messiah.

The Judgment of God (Chaps. 1–39)

In the first half of the book, Isaiah announces the coming judgment against Judah as well as the surrounding nations. No one, especially the nation He has called to be holy, can reject God without facing His just punishment. But read closely. Even the message of judgment is seasoned with the promise that God will comfort and care for His own.

Judgment against Judah (Chaps. 1–12)

Since judgment begins with the household of God (see 1 Pet. 4:17), it's no surprise that the first twelve chapters focus on Judah's condemnation.

God first communicated to Isaiah that His people had "revolted" (1:2) against Him. Judah is compared to a broken body (v. 6), unprotected by the God they had turned away from, and a harlot (v. 21), faithless to the God they had covenanted with. Instead of obeying Him, the people, even the leaders, had turned to selfishly satisfying their own needs and passions.

The nation continued to exercise a form of religion (vv. 10–15), but this only increased their guilt—God knew the violence and oppression that it belied. He knew their hearts were not in their worship, and it was their hearts that He wanted.

The nation of Israel, the "vineyard" God had lovingly planted, had produced worthless grapes, that is, sinful works (5:2–4; see also 3:14). As judgment, God would allow the vineyard to be trampled. In the immediate context, this would depict the northern kingdom's fall to Assyria. But it also foreshadowed Judah's fall under Babylon's Nebuchadnezzar.

Whom would God send to pierce the spiritual darkness of Judah with His holy light? Isaiah. But first, He had to make Isaiah aware of his own guilt—and of God's atoning grace (6:1–7). The Lord allowed the prophet a glimpse of His awesome glory and power.

Juxtaposed against God's white-hot holiness, Isaiah clearly saw the darkness of his own sinfulness and that of his people. God, however, cleansed him from his sin. Now he was ready to tell Judah about a holy God who not only judges sin but also forgives those who repent and turn to Him. Isaiah's task wouldn't be easy; God assured him that the people's hearts would harden upon hearing the message (vv. 8–13).

Chapters 7–12 predict Judah's impending judgment as well as refer repeatedly to the Messiah, who will rescue His people from sin and eventually set up His kingdom on earth.

7:14

"Therefore the Lord Himself will give you a sign:
Behold, a virgin will be with child and bear a son,
and she will call His name Immanuel." . . .

9:6-7

For a child will be born to us, a son will
be given to us;
And the government will rest on His shoul-
ders;
And His name will be called Wonderful
Counselor, Mighty God,
Eternal Father, Prince of Peace.
There will be no end to the increase of
His government or of peace,
On the throne of David and over his king-
dom,
To establish it and to uphold it with jus-
tice and righteousness
From then on and forevermore.
The zeal of the Lord of hosts will accom-
plish this.
(7:14; 9:6–7; see also 9:2; 11:1–4; 12:1–3)

Judgment against the Nations (Chaps. 13–23)

Judah had no corner on the sin market. The surrounding nations had also sinned against God. They had worshiped idols and disdained God's covenant people. So God pronounced judgment against Babylon, Assyria, Philistia, Moab, Syria, Ethiopia, Egypt, Edom, Arabia, and Tyre. But in the midst of these judgments, Jerusalem came in for a scathing rebuke; she was blind in the "valley of vision" (22:5), foolishly saying, "Let us eat and drink, for tomorrow we may die" (22:13).

The Day of the Lord (Chaps. 24–27)

This section has been called "Isaiah's Apocalypse," because it deals with Christ's second coming and His final victory over the forces of evil. Also, in terrifying images, it describes the tribulations His people will experience before He returns to set up His kingdom on earth.

Why Isaiah jumped so far ahead in history at this point is uncertain. Perhaps he wanted to emphasize that God's judgment of Judah and the surrounding nations was just a foretaste of God's eventual destruction of all evil.

Judgment and Blessing (Chaps. 28–35)

The theme of judgment continues as God declares through Isaiah six "woes" against both Israel and Judah for specific sins (chaps. 28–33). Chief among the sins of both northern and southern kingdoms was their putting trust in wealth and foreign alliances instead of in the living God.

This section concludes with another pronouncement of God's judgment against the nations and the promise of coming blessing in God's kingdom.

Historical Interlude (Chaps. 36–39)

Why, in the midst of all the woes and reassurances of prophecy, did Isaiah stop to record these episodes from Hezekiah's reign? If we read the flow of events in these chapters carefully, we'll discover the reason.

The preceding chapters have as their historical backdrop the fall of the northern kingdom to Assyria. When we enter chapters 36–39, this section puts us right in the middle of Assyria's rapacious attack on Judah. Sennacherib, king of Assyria, not satisfied to have destroyed Israel, had threatened to invade Jerusalem. Hezekiah went to the temple to call on the Lord for protection, and God miraculously defeated Sennacherib's army. The Assyrian king returned to his homeland, where, in the temple of his god, he was later murdered by his own sons.

Sometime during Sennacherib's threat, Hezekiah developed a deadly illness. Judah's good king again turned to the Lord for help, and God added fifteen years to his life.

Eventually, however, Hezekiah became self-impressed, priding himself on his own wealth and accomplishments. When the king of Babylon (Merodach-baladan at that time) sent envoys to congratulate Hezekiah on his recovery from illness, Hezekiah gave them a grand tour of his royal riches and armory. By touting his power, Hezekiah might have been trying to recruit Babylon as an ally against Assyria.

Isaiah rebuked the king, warning him not to trust in his wealth, for one day all of it "'shall be carried to Babylon; nothing shall be left,' says the Lord" (39:6). This was, of course, the prediction of Nebuchadnezzar's invasion and eventual destruction of Jerusalem in 586 B.C., still more than one hundred years away.

This historical interlude, then, bridges the Assyrian demolition of Israel and Babylon's ruin of Judah. As we move into the next section, Isaiah's prophecies turn to encouragement and consolation in the wake of the Babylonian exile.

The Deliverance of God (Chaps. 40–66)

Chapter 40 transports us to the future, to the waning days of Judah's exile in Babylon, allowing us a glimpse into the fulfillment of God's promise that Judah would be taken captive. This second division of the book focuses on God's deliverance of and His comfort and care for His people. It also presents the ultimate Deliverer, Jesus Christ.

The Supremacy of the Lord (Chaps. 40–48)

Authors Bruce Wilkinson and Kenneth Boa summarize these chapters this way:

> Having pronounced Judah's divine condemnation, Isaiah comforts them with God's promises of hope and restoration. The basis for this hope is the sovereignty and majesty of God (40–48). Of the 216 verses in these nine chapters, 115 speak of God's greatness and power. The Creator is contrasted with idols, the creations of men. His sovereign character is Judah's assurance of future restoration. Babylon will indeed carry them off; but Babylon will finally be judged and destroyed, and God's people will be released from captivity.[4]

4. Wilkinson and Boa, *Talk Thru the Old Testament,* p. 194.

And so we're reminded there is more to God's character than judgment. He is full of mercy and grace, eager to lavish His love on His people—even after He has punished them for disobedience. Listen to the tenderness of His heart:

> "Comfort, O comfort My people," says your God.
> "Speak kindly to Jerusalem;
> And call out to her, that her warfare has ended,
> That her iniquity has been removed,
> That she has received of the Lord's hand
> Double for all her sins." ' . . .
> Like a shepherd He will tend His flock,
> In His arm He will gather the lambs,
> And carry them in His bosom;
> He will gently lead the nursing ewes.
> (40:1–2, 11)

The Servant of the Lord (Chaps. 49–53)

God's mercy and love are revealed most fully in the person of Christ, foreshadowed in Isaiah as the Servant of the Lord. He will come to suffer for His people, securing their salvation. He will also be "a light for the Gentiles," so that He will bring God's "salvation to the ends of the earth" (49:6 NIV).

In this section, the predictive portrait of Christ's suffering is amazing in its detail and fulfillment in the Gospels. We see Him beaten (50:6; 52:14), silent before His oppressors (53:7), "a man of sorrows, and acquainted with grief" (v. 3). "He Himself bore the sin of many, And interceded for the transgressors" (v. 12). Freed from sin and at peace with God, His people can rejoice,

> How lovely on the mountains
> Are the feet of him who brings good news,
> Who announces peace
> And brings good news of happiness,
> Who announces salvation,
> And says to Zion, "Your God reigns!" (52:7)

The Future Plan of the Lord (Chaps. 54–66)

With His people redeemed, ransomed with something more precious than money, the Messiah will one day return to establish His kingdom of peace on earth. All who come to Him believing in His salvation will be welcome, whether Jew or Gentile: "My house will be called a house of prayer for all the peoples" (56:7). Righteousness and justice will flourish; and if they are not upheld, God will judge His enemies. "'There is no peace,' says my God, 'for the wicked'"—a refrain that emphasizes God's holy standard (57:21; see also 48:22). At last, He will bless His people and make all things new.

Isaiah may have been "Prince among Prophets." But even greater than the man was his message—news of new life, new hope, and a new world under the King of Kings and Lord of Lords.

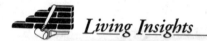 *Living Insights*

"Here am I. Send me!"

The latter portion of Isaiah 6:8 is often quoted as an admonition for Christians to make themselves available for missionary work. There's more to spreading the gospel, however, than just being available, as the greater context of Isaiah 6 shows us.

Before Isaiah could go, he had to grieve—over his sin, over the sins of his nation, over the infinite gulf that lay between himself and a holy God. Before he could be sent, he had to be cleansed.

Christ has commissioned us to take the gospel message to the world (Matt. 28:18–20). But spreading the true gospel requires knowing the true God—all of His attributes, from His consuming holiness to His cleansing grace. We must balance the going with the knowing. In fact, we're not really ready to go until we know.

The closer we get to God, and the more we come to grips with what He has done for us in Christ, the harder it is to keep Him to ourselves. Knowing God. That's where evangelism and missions begin.

Chapter 11

JEREMIAH: WEEPING, WARNING, AND WAITING

A Survey of Jeremiah

> "And when the people ask, 'Why has the Lord our God done all this to us?' you will tell them, 'As you have forsaken me and served foreign gods in your own land, so now you will serve foreigners in a land not your own.'" (Jer. 5:19 NIV)

W hen we hear from God, it isn't always good news; it doesn't always cheer us up or fit into our plans. Sometimes God's truth is more than we want to hear and difficult to swallow. It often mixes pain with pleasure, blessings with curses. It confronts us, rattles us, slams against our comfort zone, and forces us to face what's important.

Delivering God's truth isn't always easy, either. It often means raining on parades, reminding others how far they have drifted from God. And that can make you unpopular. It made Jeremiah unpopular—he was threatened, beaten, put in stocks, and imprisoned. But he stood strong and delivered God's message, because he loved Him and he loved His people. He knew they needed to hear the hard things God had to say to them. In those days of impending judgment, to listen was to live.

Background

The Conditions in Judah

Twenty-five years after the Northern Kingdom of Israel fell to Assyria, Manasseh took the throne of Judah. Under his infamous fifty-five year rule, Judah rejected Hezekiah's godly legacy and headed full-bore into apostasy, idolatry, and moral decay. This worst of Judah's kings had "shed very much innocent blood until he had filled Jerusalem from one end to another" (2 Kings 21:16). Judah became as wicked as her sister, Israel, until Manasseh's grandson took the throne.

Josiah, the boy-king and Judah's last good monarch, began to actively seek the Lord when he was sixteen; and at twenty, he purged Judah and Jerusalem of all her idolatrous trappings

JEREMIAH

Judah's Sin and Judgment		Prophecies against the Nations		A Sobering Ending
Jeremiah's Call	**Exhortations to Judah**	Egypt	Damascus	Jerusalem in ruins
Idolatry	Promises of restoration (30–33)	Philistia	Kedar & Hazor	
Corrupt leadership	Fall of Jerusalem and aftermath (39–45)	Moab	Elam	
Moral compromise		Ammon	Babylon	
		Edom		
CHAPTERS 1–45		*CHAPTERS 46–51*		*CHAPTER 52*

Key Verses	7:23–24; 8:11–12, 21; 9: 23–24; ch. 31
Theme	Judgment is coming; repent!
Christ in Jeremiah	The Spring of Living Water (2:13); the Righteous Branch, Coming Shepherd, The Lord Our Righteousness (23:5–6); the New Covenant (ch. 31); Redeemer (50:34)

(2 Chron. 34:1–7). The next year, 627 B.C., Jeremiah was called by God to be His prophet (Jer. 1:2). Then, five years after that, a crucial discovery was made. While purifying the Lord's temple, Josiah's servants found the sacred book of the Law—God's covenant with His people given through Moses (2 Chron. 34:8–28).

Revival swept through the land, due to Josiah's heartfelt devotion to God. Josiah and all the people of Judah renewed the covenant with their Lord, and the young king had the nation celebrate the greatest Passover since Samuel's time (34:29–35:19). Spiritually, the troubled nation looked as though it was finally back on track. And politically, the next ten years saw Judah's old nemesis Assyria overthrown by a newer power, Babylon, in 612 B.C. Everything seemed to be looking up. Until Josiah's untimely death at age thirty-nine in a futile fight against Egypt (35:20–24).

Jeremiah lamented the passing of this great and godly king, this kindred spirit in the Lord (v. 25). And he lamented the future of Judah and Jerusalem without him. With Josiah's son Jehoahaz taken in chains to Egypt and Pharaoh Neco renaming and installing another of Josiah's sons, Jehoiakim, on the throne, the nation soon reverted to idolatry and corruption (2 Kings 23:31–37). The bleak vision of Judah's downfall given by Isaiah was less than forty years from becoming reality (Isa. 39:5–7).

Now only Jeremiah and Habakkuk spoke for God, warning the fickle people of approaching judgment and desperately calling them to turn back to God.

The Call of Jeremiah

Jeremiah, son of Hilkiah, a priest at Anothoth, was commissioned by God like John the Baptizer and Jesus—long before he was born.

> Now the word of the Lord came to me saying,
> "Before I formed you in the womb I knew you,
> And before you were born I consecrated you;
> I have appointed you a prophet to the nations."
> (Jer. 1:4–5)

What a staggering, thrilling, sure calling! Before we get too excited, though, we need to see what else the Lord told Jeremiah.

"They will fight against you." (1:19)

"You shall speak all these words to them, but they

will not listen to you; and you shall call to them, but they will not answer you." (7:27)

The people's determined resistance, however, would break the prophet's heart.

> A heart-broken prophet with a heart-breaking message, Jeremiah labors for more than forty years proclaiming a message of doom to the stiff-necked people of Judah. Despised and persecuted by his countrymen, Jeremiah bathes his harsh prophecies in tears of compassion. His broken heart causes him to write a broken book, which is difficult to arrange chronologically or topically. But through his sermons and signs he faithfully declares that surrender to God's will is the only way to escape calamity.[1]

Jeremiah didn't mince words. On occasion, he even

> engaged in calling for redress against his personal enemies (12:1–3; 15:15; 17:18; 18:19–23)—a practice that explains the origin of the English word "jeremiad," referring to a denunciatory tirade or complaint.[2]

Jeremiah ministered during the reigns of five kings of Judah: Josiah, Jehoahaz, Jehoiakim, Jehoiachin, and Zedekiah—Judah's last king. Jeremiah was a contemporary of four other prophets: Zephaniah, Habakkuk, Daniel, and Ezekiel.

His ministry, then, can be divided into three stages: "(1) From 627 to 605 B.C. he prophesied while Judah was threatened by Assyria and Egypt. (2) From 605 to 586 B.C. he proclaimed God's judgment while Judah was threatened and besieged by Babylon. (3) From 586 to about 580 B.C. he ministered in Jerusalem and Egypt after Judah's downfall."[3]

The Characteristics and Structure of the Book

Jeremiah is the longest book in the Bible, containing more

1. Bruce Wilkinson and Kenneth Boa, *Talk Thru the Old Testament*, vol. 1 of *Talk Thru the Bible* (Nashville, Tenn.: Thomas Nelson Publishers, 1983), p. 198.

2. Ronald Youngblood, introduction to Jeremiah, in *The NIV Study Bible*, ed. Kenneth Barker and others (Grand Rapids, Mich.: Zondervan Bible Publishers, 1985), p. 1115.

3. Wilkinson and Boa, *Talk Thru the Old Testament*, p. 199.

words than any other book. Another challenging fact is that it is not arranged chronologically. However, it is easy to enter into and get caught up in the prophet's passion because he arranged his messages logically.

> As Jeremiah compiled his subsequent collections of his prophecies, he rearranged them in a logical pattern. The arrangement developed his theme of God's judgment. Chapters 2–45 focused on God's judgment on Judah and chapters 46–51 focused on God's judgment on the Gentile nations.[4]

This arrangement keeps the book moving and active, as does the mix of poetry and narration.

We can divide the book according to the development of Jeremiah's judgment theme. Chapter 1 introduces Jeremiah and the grim task of confrontational ministry that lies ahead of him. Chapters 2–45 focus on prophecies related to Judah. Chapters 46–51 proclaim judgment against the nations. The final chapter, 52, describes the last days of Jerusalem and the fate of the people.

A Reluctant Recruit (Chap. 1)

In Josiah's thirteenth year as king, Jeremiah received his predestined call from God (1:4–5). Like Moses, however (see Exod. 3:10–11), Jeremiah was hesitant to take on the job of God's spokesman. "Alas, Lord God! Behold, I do not know how to speak, Because I am a youth," he protested (Jer. 1:6). But God took his eyes off the one being sent and put them back on the One doing the sending (vv. 7–9).

Just what kind of ministry had the Lord called him to?

> "See, I have appointed you this day over the
>   nations and over the kingdoms,
> To pluck up and to break down,
> To destroy and to overthrow,
> To build and to plant." (v. 10)

Jeremiah would proclaim a violent word of the Lord—a word of scalding judgment soon to come from Babylon (vv. 11–16).

---

4. Charles H. Dyer, "Jeremiah," in *The Bible Knowledge Commentary*, Old Testament edition, ed. John F. Walvoord and Roy B. Zuck (Wheaton, Ill.: Scripture Press Publications, Victor Books, 1985), p. 1128.

There would be hope interspersed with the prophecies; but overall, his was not an enviable task. The Lord promised, though, that He would be with Jeremiah and give him strength to pronounce His judgments in the face of opposition (vv. 18–19).

Sinfulness of and Prophecies about Judah (Chaps. 2–45)

The main section of Jeremiah's book delineates the sins of Judah and declares God's coming judgment against her. He includes an interlude of hope and restoration; but only five chapters later, we read the most thorough account of Jerusalem's fall recorded in Scripture. Jeremiah communicated God's messages through a variety of poignant means: poetry, parables, sermons, and object lessons.

A Litany of Lawlessness (Chaps. 2–29)

Lest there be any doubt that God's judgment of Judah was just, Jeremiah listed the various ways the nation has sinned against Him: idolatry, spiritual adultery, not defending the fatherless and poor, oppression, violence, destruction, greed, deceit, slander, empty rituals and worship, profaning the Lord's house with their corrupt lives, child sacrifice, unfaithfulness, plotting evil, shedding innocent blood. Those in leadership respected their own authority more than God's, and the prophets prophesied lies. The people rejected God's Law and broke His covenant. Prophets and priests gave the people a false sense of security, saying "'Peace, peace,'" as if God would sanction their idolatry and injustice by granting them peace (8:11). The people, God complained, "weary themselves committing iniquity" (9:5).

Because of the people's stubborn-hearted sins, God would "make Jerusalem a heap of ruins, A haunt of jackals; and . . . the cities of Judah a desolation, without inhabitant" (v. 11). But He left the door open for repentance: "Wash your heart from evil, O Jerusalem, That you may be saved. How long will your wicked thoughts Lodge within you?" (4:14).

Jeremiah's emotions and life became entwined with his message. He struggled and questioned God's judgments at times (12:1–4; 15:15–18; 20:7–18). And God made his life an object lesson for the people. He did not allow Jeremiah to marry or console the mourning or rejoice with those who celebrated, for He wanted to show the nation how comfortless their existence would be once He withdrew His blessing from them (16:1–9).

Jeremiah's prophecies, of course, met much resistance. Nobody wants to have their sins read in the public square, and no one wants to believe that disaster is coming when life seems so good. But Jeremiah would not be silenced. His life was threatened by the people of his own hometown (11:18–23); he was beaten and put in stocks (20:1–2); and he was nearly killed by the priests, prophets, and people at the Lord's house (chap. 26).

Still, he pressed on, using a variety of visual aids to get God's message across. A linen belt, buried in the ground and ruined, represented the ruin of Israel and Judah, once bound close to the Lord (13:1–11). Full wineskins symbolized the fullness of God's wrath (vv. 12–14). A visit to the potter's house reinforced the message that God was the potter and Judah the clay, to be done with as God deemed fit (18:1–10). A smashed jar symbolized the smashing of Judah (chap. 19). Two baskets of figs conveyed two messages: the good figs represented those already exiled in the first two deportations; the spoiled figs, those still in Jerusalem, whom the Lord would destroy (chap. 24). By wearing a yoke, Jeremiah embodied the message that the Jews should serve Nebuchadnezzar (chap. 27).

Jeremiah wept over his countrymen, but he must have been comforted knowing that God would one day redeem a portion of His people for Himself (23:3–8; 24:6–7). In fact, he wrote a letter to those who had already been taken to Babylon, encouraging them to build a life and prosper there, for God would watch over them and bring them back to the land seventy years later (chap. 29).

An Interlude of Hope (Chaps. 30–33)

As a testament to His good faith, God instructed Jeremiah to perform another object lesson: he was to buy a field to show that "houses and fields and vineyards shall again be bought in this land" (32:15). "I have loved you with an everlasting love," the Lord pledged to His people; "Again I will build you, and you shall be rebuilt" (31:3a, 4a).

Not only would God bring the Jews back to the land, He would establish a new covenant with them. This new covenant, as the editors of *Eerdmans Handbook of the Bible* write,

> would replace the old one made at Sinai, which they had broken. This time God will remake them from within, giving them the power to do his will (31:31–34; and compare Romans 8:1–4;

2 Corinthians 5:17). Like Isaiah before him, Jeremiah here telescopes future events. He is talking, in the short-term, of the actual return from exile; in the long-term he looks forward to the new covenant brought in by Christ himself (see Hebrews 8ff.).[5]

Hardened Hearts and a Nation's Fall (Chaps. 34–45)

Chapters 34–38 compose a mosaic of vacillation and contemptuous resistance. King Zedekiah freed all the slaves in Jerusalem, but soon afterward he and the people reneged on their agreement and enslaved them again—a direct violation of God's Law (see Deut. 15:12–15, 18). Jehoiakim defiantly burned a scroll containing all the prophecies God had given Jeremiah (36:23). And angry officials had the prophet beaten and thrown into a dungeon, with Zedekiah "rescuing" him by imprisoning him in the court of the guardhouse (chap. 37). Later, a more indifferent Zedekiah allowed Jeremiah to be confined in a deep, muddy cistern. Only by the mercy of an official named Ebed-melech did Jeremiah escape that and return to the guardhouse, where he would remain until Jerusalem's fall (chap. 38).

Jerusalem fell in 586 B.C. (chap. 39). Zedekiah tried to escape, coward that he was, but was captured. Nebuchadnezzar killed his two sons then had Zedekiah blinded, bound, and carried to Babylon. Then the Babylonians burned Jerusalem to the ground, exiling all but the poorest people. Nebuzaradan, commander of Babylon's imperial guard, freed Jeremiah and offered him a post in Babylon. Unlike Zedekiah, Jeremiah bravely chose to remain in Jerusalem (39:11–40:6).

After the exile, Gedaliah, the governor Babylon appointed over Judah, was assassinated by some disgruntled Jews (40:7–41:15). The people, fearing reprisals from Nebuchadnezzar, fled to Egypt, despite Jeremiah's prophecies not to (41:16–42:22). Even with the stench of a burning Jerusalem still in their nostrils, the people of Judah rejected God. They went to Egypt anyway, taking Jeremiah and Baruch, his secretary, with them against their will (43:1–7). And they worshiped Egyptian gods, despite Jeremiah's prophetic warnings (43:8–44:30). A preexilic message to Baruch completes this

---

5. David and Pat Alexander, eds., *Eerdmans Handbook to the Bible* (1973; reprint, Grand Rapids, Mich.: William B. Eerdmans Publishing Co., 1983), p. 405.

section, capturing the exiles' pain and God's word to them by way of Baruch (chap. 45). We can't be certain what happened to Jeremiah in Egypt, but tradition says he was stoned to death there.

Prophecies against the Nations (Chaps. 46–51)

We might title this section "poetic justice." In vivid verse, these chapters remind us that God is sovereign over all nations, not just Judah and Israel. Just as Isaiah had prophesied before him, Jeremiah promised that the evil of the nations surrounding Judah had not gone unnoticed.

Egypt, Philistia, Moab, Ammon, Edom, Damascus, Kedar, Hazor, Elam, and Babylon (which received the longest denunciation—two chapters) would all face God's judgment for their pride, idolatry, and abuse of God's people.

A Sobering Ending (Chap. 52)

Jeremiah's book ends by vindicating its author, showing that the Word of the Lord was true all along. Jerusalem was ravaged, the temple raided and burned, and the people taken away in chains.

The last few verses offer a hint that the Jews would not remain in exile forever. Jehoiachin was released from prison in Babylon, invited to dine with the king, and supported financially. Indeed, God was not at all finished with His people. But that truth couldn't keep Jeremiah from weeping over all they had lost.

 *Living Insights*

Having just read about Jerusalem's fall, we might be tempted to think that God enjoys doing harm to His people. He punishes sin, that's for sure. But that's not what gives Him joy (see Lam. 3:33). He actually *delights* in doing us good. Want proof?

> "And I will make an everlasting covenant with them that I will not turn away from them, to do them good; and I will put the fear of Me in their hearts so that they will not turn away from Me. And I will rejoice over them to do them good, and I will faithfully plant them in this land with all My heart and with all My soul." (Jer. 32:40–41)

This promise, of course, was given to the exiled Jews. But when we combine this passage with others from the New Testament (Rom. 8:28–39, for example), we know that when God chooses a people for Himself—including Christians today—they are His forever. And, though He sometimes disciplines them, they are forever the objects of His perfect love.

Is that how you see God? As Someone who has determined to do good to you and love you forever? Or is He more like a cosmic mugger, lurking around a dark corner, waiting to jump you and rob you of life's joy?

Indeed, God is righteous, holy, pure, and perfect. And as such, He must punish evil. But for those who have put their trust in Christ, God is our Benefactor, our Father, our Friend. By taking our place on the cross, Jesus removed all obstacles that would keep us from receiving and relishing God's love.

God's love isn't some fickle thing that fluctuates with moods or environment. It is constant. It is aggressive. It is eternal. Listen to the words of John Piper:

> Many people have no personal experience of knowing that they were loved by God eternally and will be cared for by him with omnipotent, all-supplying love for ever and ever. Many people think of God's love only in terms of a love that offers and waits, but does not take us for himself and work with infinite enthusiasm to keep us and glorify us forever. Yet this is the experience available for any who will come and drink the water of life freely (Revelation 22:17).[6]

With infinite enthusiasm! That's how God loves us. Here are a few more passages that speak of God's love and goodness toward us. Read. Reflect. And return to these when you feel unloved.

Psalm 23	Romans 8:28–39
Psalm 84:11	Ephesians 2:4–10
Jeremiah 31:3	1 John 4:19

God delights in giving His love. Shouldn't we delight in receiving it?

---

6. John Piper, *The Pleasures of God* (Portland, Oreg.: Multnomah Press, 1991), p. 148.

Chapter 12

LAMENTATIONS: A PROPHET'S BROKEN HEART

A Survey of Lamentations

The smoke rises in misty tendrils, like wisps of ghosts slipping from their graves. It hovers over the charred ruins, shrouding the broken city in a gray, appalling stillness. It seeps into the throat, lungs, and eyes—stinging with yesterday's terror and today's utter desolation.

Burned . . . all burned. Solomon's holy temple, the king's stately palace. Every house, every important building rich with history. Burned to the ground. Jerusalem's hope, Jerusalem's future reduced to smoking rubble. She seems as feeble and frail as her toppled walls, its stones strewn far and near.

The weeping prophet, his warning message so long spurned, himself so often abused, tenderly takes his people's anguish to his heart and composes a dirge with his tears.

> How lonely sits the city
> That was full of people!
> She has become like a widow
> Who was once great among the nations!
> She who was a princess among the provinces
> Has become a forced laborer!
> She weeps bitterly in the night,
> And her tears are on her cheeks;
> She has none to comfort her. (Lam. 1:1–2a)

How the prophet did not want the city's doom. How he longed and prayed for the people to return to their God. But they would not. And now he laments the lost glory of Israel, mourns for the pain of a judged people. In his cry is heard that of One who would weep over the people's stubborn hearts centuries later.

> "O Jerusalem, Jerusalem, who kills the prophets and stones those who are sent to her! How often I wanted to gather your children together, the way a hen gathers her chicks under her wings, and you were unwilling. Behold, your house is being left to you desolate!" (Matt. 23:37–38)

LAMENTATIONS

	Jerusalem's Desolation	The Lord's Anger	Jeremiah's Grief	The Lord's Anger	Jeremiah's Prayer
	CHAPTER 1	CHAPTER 2	CHAPTER 3	CHAPTER 4	CHAPTER 5
Underlying Emotion	Lonely, groaning	Angry, exhorting	Broken, weeping	Desperate, anguished	Weary, pleading
Key Verses	1:1, 5	2:14, 17	3:16–24	4:11–12	5:5, 19–22
Short Prayers	1:20–22 "See us!"	2:20–22 "Look at us!"	3:55–66 "Judge them!"	4:20 "Avenge us!"	5:21 "Restore us!"
Main Theme	Mourning over sin; the severity of God's judgment; hope in His mercy				
Christ in Lamentations	Jesus, like Jeremiah, wept over the sins of Jerusalem (Matt. 23:27–38; Luke 13:34–35).				

Even God Himself weeps at His people's tragic choices, as Jesus' words and Jeremiah's inspired pen reveal.

Background of the Book

Lamentations has been called "perhaps the saddest book of the Old Testament."[1] Though it contains one of the best known passages of hope in the entire Bible, it is, as a whole, "a funeral service for the death of the city."[2]

To enter into the grieving Jeremiah's sorrow more fully, let's gain an understanding of the background, structure, and style of his book.

Name

From the first word in chapters 1, 2, and 4 came the original Hebrew title: *ekah*, which can be translated either "Alas!" or "How!" Though this captured the emotion of the book, another word, *qinot*, meaning "dirges" or "laments," more precisely represented its substance. The Greek Septuagint and Latin Vulgate translated this second title and also followed Jewish tradition in ascribing the work to Jeremiah. Down through the centuries, then, this book has been known as The Lamentations of Jeremiah.[3]

Author and Date

Though no author is named, the similarities between Jeremiah's prophecies and the language used in Lamentations build a strong case for Jeremiah's authorship. Many of the same phrases and metaphors are used in both books, such as:

- "terror(s) on every side" (Jer. 6:25; 20:10; 46:5; 49:29; Lam. 2:22)

- the yoke (Jer. 27–28; Lam. 1:14)

- weeping (Jer. 9:1; 13:17; 14:17a; Lam. 1:16; 2:11, 18; 3:48–49)

- an incurable woundedness (Jer. 10:19; 14:17b; 15:18; 30:12–15; Lam. 2:13)

1. Bruce Wilkinson and Kenneth Boa, *Talk Thru the Old Testament*, vol. 1 of *Talk Thru the Bible* (Nashville, Tenn.: Thomas Nelson Publishers, 1983), p. 206.

2. Eugene H. Peterson, *Five Smooth Stones for Pastoral Work* (Atlanta, Ga.: John Knox Press, 1980), p. 95.

3. Charles H. Dyer, "Lamentations," in *The Bible Knowledge Commentary*, Old Testament edition, ed. John F. Walvoord and Roy B. Zuck (Wheaton, Ill.: Scripture Press Publications, Victor Books, 1985), p. 1207.

- the betrayal of "lovers" or allies (Jer. 30:14; Lam. 1:2)

Jeremiah also was known for writing laments (see 2 Chron. 35:25). Further, the writer of Lamentations had to have been an eyewitness to the Babylonian siege and final conquest in order to portray it with such painful clarity, and Jeremiah experienced it all (Jer. 39–40). Most likely, Jeremiah wrote his five laments shortly after Jerusalem's destruction in 586 B.C., possibly during Gedaliah's governorship (Jer. 40:5–16).

Bruce Wilkinson and Kenneth Boa summarize Jeremiah's couplet of books this way: Jeremiah is *warning*, while Lamentations is *mourning*. The prophecies looked ahead, while the laments look back.[4]

Structure and Style

Lamentations, like Psalms, is composed not of chapters but of individual poems. But where the book of Psalms is a collection of diverse poems written over the ages, the five poems in Lamentations comprise a single, unified book. Wilkinson and Boa call it "a five-poem dirge."[5]

The first four of these funeral laments have a particular meter, called *qinah*, or "limping meter." Charles Dyer explains that "in this rhythmic pattern the second half of a line of verse has one less beat than the first half of a line. This . . . conveys a hollow, incomplete feeling to the reader," which lends "an air of sadness to the dirges and heighten[s] their emotional intensity."[6]

Another crucial part of Lamentations' structure is its acrostic form. The first four laments were written to correspond to the twenty-two letters of the Hebrew alphabet. Each verse of chapters 1, 2, and 4 follows the Hebrew alphabet; chapter 3, which is sixty-six verses long, has three verses per letter; while chapter 5 is not an acrostic, nor does it have the same metrical pattern, it has the same twenty-two verse length.

Acrostics were often used in the Psalms and Proverbs as memory aids, but there seems to be a more significant reason for the use of this structure in Lamentations. Perhaps it was a way to contain and sort through the inner chaos that suffering creates. Eugene Peterson brings great insight to this literary device.

4. Wilkinson and Boa, *Talk Thru the Old Testament*, p. 209.

5. Wilkinson and Boa, *Talk Thru the Old Testament*, p. 207.

6. Dyer, "Lamentations," p. 1210.

The acrostic patiently, and carefully, goes through the letters of the alphabet and covers the ground of suffering. Every detail of suffering comes under consideration.

One of the commonest ways to deal with another's suffering is to make light of it, to gloss it over, to attempt shortcuts through it. Because it is so painful, we try to get to the other side quickly. Lamentations provides a structure to guarantee against that happening.[7]

Lamentations explores the experience of suffering with completeness, from A to Z. Suffering is expressed thoroughly—told five times, in fact. Peterson concludes:

In such ways does the acrostic function: it organizes grief, patiently going over the ground, step by step, insisting on the significance of each detail of suffering. The pain is labeled—defined and objectified. Arranged in the acrostic structure the suffering no longer obsesses, no longer controls. The rough rhythm of the *kinah* meter expressing the inner anarchy is patiently arranged in an order which becomes a work of art.[8]

The fifth lament, which is a prayer, does not use the limping meter, acrostic, or "How" beginning. Exhausted with grief, it quietly lays the pain before God and pleas for His restoration.

The book as a whole also has a deliberate structural balance. Charles Dyer observes that "chapters 1–2 and 4–5 parallel each other." He elaborates:

Chapters 1 and 5 focus on the people while chapters 2 and 4 focus on the Lord. Chapter 3 provides the pivot for the book, pointing to Jeremiah's response in the midst of affliction.[9]

Use

In the Hebrew Scriptures, Lamentations was one of the five

7. Peterson, *Five Smooth Stones*, p. 97.

8. Peterson, *Five Smooth Stones*, pp. 99–100.

9. Dyer, "Lamentations," p. 1211.

Megilloth, or "rolls," that were read publicly at annual Jewish festivals. The Song of Solomon was read at Passover; Ruth, at Pentecost; Ecclesiastes, at the Feast of Tabernacles; Esther at Purim; and Lamentations, at a fast on the ninth of Ab—to commemorate Jerusalem's fall in 586 B.C. and her second destruction in A.D. 70.[10]

Survey of Lamentations

"Since my people are crushed, I am crushed," moaned Jeremiah (Jer. 8:21 NIV). Let us sit beside him and take to our hearts the anguish he took to his.

Chapter 1: Jerusalem's Desolation

"How lonely sits the city That was full of people!" is the opening wail of pain (Lam. 1:1). Judah has gone into exile; a noble people have become slaves. The allies she had counted on have abandoned her; her friends and lovers have become enemies. "She has none to comfort her" is the desolate, echoing refrain (vv. 2, 9, 16, 17, 21).

For eleven verses, Jeremiah describes Judah's destruction because of her sins (vv. 1–11). "For the Lord has caused her grief," he writes, "Because of the multitude of her transgressions. . . . She did not consider her future; Therefore she has fallen astonishingly" (vv. 5, 9). Then, in the next eleven verses, personified Jerusalem tells of her suffering and how her enemies mock her (vv. 12–22). Laid low by judgment, this first lament ends bleakly, "For my groans are many, and my heart is faint" (v. 22).

Chapter 2: The Lord's Anger

"How the Lord has covered the daughter of Zion With a cloud in His anger!" (2:1). Temple, sanctuary, and altar are torn down; the walls of the city, toppled; the law and prophets, gone. In a frightening display of His holy wrath, the Lord has "thrown down," "cut off," "burned in Jacob like a flaming fire," "poured out His wrath," "swallowed up Israel," "destroyed," "rejected," "despised," and "abandoned" (vv. 1–8). Children starve, enemies taunt, and the tears of God's people "run down like a river day and night" (v. 18). The Lord's unsparing, pitiless anger permeates this lament (vv. 2, 17, 21).

---

10. See J. Sidlow Baxter, *Explore the Book*, 6 vols. in 1 (Grand Rapids, Mich.: Zondervan Publishing House, Academie Books, 1966), vol. 3, p. 280; Peterson, *Five Smooth Stones*, p. 95; Wilkinson and Boa, *Talk Thru the Old Testament*, p. 209.

Chapter 3: Jeremiah's Grief

"I am the man who has seen affliction," Jeremiah groans, "Because of the rod of His wrath" (3:1). So intense is the prophet's suffering that he describes God's actions toward him as "a bear lying in wait," "a lion in hiding," that "dragged [him] from the path and mangled" him (vv. 10–11 NIV).

Yet in the midst of his pain, he grasps hope:

> The Lord's lovingkindnesses indeed never cease,
> For His compassions never fail.
> They are new every morning;
> Great is Thy faithfulness.
> "The Lord is my portion," says my soul,
> "Therefore I have hope in Him."
> The Lord is good to those who wait for Him,
> To the person who seeks Him.
> It is good that he waits silently
> For the salvation of the Lord. . . .
> For if He causes grief,
> Then He will have compassion
> According to His abundant lovingkindness.
> For He does not afflict willingly,
> Or grieve the sons of men. (vv. 22–26, 32–33)

From this high point of hope, Jeremiah gradually descends— seeing the injustice of his people, then urging their repentance and return to the Lord, then spiraling down in a jeremiad against his enemies. It's as if a hand of hope had reached through his darkness, but the waves of pain broke his grip.

Chapter 4: The Lord's Anger

"How the gold has lost its luster, the fine gold become dull! . . . How the precious sons of Zion, once worth their weight in gold, are now considered as pots of clay, the work of a potter's hands!" (4:1a, 2 NIV). The siege of Jerusalem is recalled here (vv. 1–10), with its scenes of starving people, some sinking to such depths as to cannibalize their own children (v. 10). Jerusalem's former glory is contrasted with her present ruin. And when Jeremiah remembers how the Lord's wrath has scattered His people, he wishes the same fate on Edom, who has rejoiced at Judah's downfall.

Chapter 5: Jeremiah's Prayer

"Remember, O Lord, what has befallen us" (5:1a). Cataloging for the final time the suffering of the rightfully judged nation, Jeremiah pleads with God for restoration. Rather than letting their guilt turn them further away from God, Jeremiah brings all their pain to Him. His sorrow is not yet abated, but his hope is in the Lord.

Concluding Observations

As we ponder the deep sorrow and devastation God's people brought on themselves, we would be wise to remember five truths about sin.

First, *sin's pleasures are often shared, but its consequences are felt individually* (note Lam. 1:2, 7, 9, 16, 17, 21). Those who continue in a lifetime of sin often experience loneliness, alienation, and isolation.

Second, *the Lord has no favorites—all who sin suffer its consequences* (note all the names for Judah in chap. 2). Not even God's chosen people were exempt from His judgment. And just because Christians are under Christ's grace today doesn't mean that God glosses over our sins. We, too, will reap what we sow (see Gal. 6:7-8).

Third, *when we experience consequences for our personal sins, there is never any reason to blame God* (note Lam. 3:34-36, 39). Our pattern of sins—our recurring choices to do what is wrong—are what brings us misery. Suffering is never the capricious undertaking of an uncaring or unjust God. Our Lord always does what is right.

Fourth, *sin's consequences bring the very things we said would never occur* (note Lam. 4:5, 7-8, 10, 12-13, 17-18, 20). "That will never happen to me!" are often famous last words. How many couples have indulged in premarital sex only to have everything changed by the conception of a baby? How many people have been taken captive by merciless addictions that began as "a harmless experiment"? Sin can bring you lower than you ever thought possible.

Fifth, *there is no misery greater than the misery following open disobedience* (note 5:2-5, 8-18). As J. Sidlow Baxter wrote, "High calling, flaunted by low living, inevitably issues in deep suffering."[11]

Is there no hope, then? With God, "the hope of Israel" (Jer. 17:13), all things are possible—even the forgiveness of the worst of sinners. Remember, "His compassions never fail. They are

---

11. Baxter, *Explore the Book*, p. 286.

new every morning. . . . He will have compassion According to His abundant lovingkindness" (Lam. 3:22b–23a, 32). Great is His faithfulness, and strong is His forgiveness (v. 23b; see also 1 John 1:9).

 *Living Insights*

Four words that never came out of the prophet Jeremiah's mouth were, "I told you so."

There was no gloating triumph, no bitter pride at being right. Just tears.

The things Jeremiah *didn't* do can teach us much. In addition to never saying, "I told you so," he also never said, "Everything is going to be alright." Because it wouldn't, not for a very long time. And even then, when the remnant would return, the rebuilt temple and city could not compare to the previous glory.

He also didn't look for a silver lining, try to make lemonade from lemons, crow about the sun coming out tomorrow. Nor did he whitewash their choices, their sins, that brought them this sorrow. Yet he didn't abandon his people either, telling them to lie in the bed they had made.

Rather, he wept honest tears, straining with the sufferers to bring all the pain to God. For He is the One who wounds but also heals, who strikes down but also lifts up (see Deut. 32:39; Job 5:18; Hos. 6:1). Since this devastation came from God's hand and not from some terribly random act of history, they could hope for comfort—hope for forgiveness. So Jeremiah stayed with these judged people, identifying with their anguish and identifying the One who could help.

When you have warned others of the likely consequences of their actions, detailed the destructive course of their decisions, how have you reacted when your predictions have come true? Let's make this a little less general and make this person your teenager or spouse. How like Jeremiah are you?

_____

_____

_____

_____

If the tables were turned and you were the one who had erred and were suffering as a result, how would you like your pain handled? How do you treat yourself?

_____

_____

_____

_____

Redemption, not retaliation or rationalization, should always be our goal. Because, when you think about it, it's always God's (compare 2 Cor. 7:10).

Chapter 13

EZEKIEL: STRONG MAN OF GOD

A *Survey of Ezekiel*

Isaiah warned. Jeremiah wept. Ezekiel went.

A prophet in exile. Seems strange, doesn't it? Why keep trying, Lord? Why raise up another spokesman? The people didn't listen to the prophets while in Jerusalem, so why send one to Babylon? Why not let the exiles lie in the bed they had made for themselves?

Because, as the psalmist explained, "The Lord is good; His lovingkindness is everlasting, And His faithfulness to all generations" (Ps. 100:5). That means God doesn't abandon His people. Even in exile, He spoke to them, confronting them with their sins and giving them hope of a restored relationship with Himself.

That's where Ezekiel comes in. As a prophet who ministered among the exiles in Babylon, he represented the voice and presence of God among a people with no temple, no holy city, no national identity. God's loving pursuit of His people knows no boundaries —geographical, cultural, or otherwise. That was true in Ezekiel's day. And it's true today.

An Introduction to the Man

As Jeremiah approached the end of his ministry in Jerusalem, warning the inhabitants about the city's impending destruction, Ezekiel was already living in Babylon as an exile. Three facts about the prophet will help us understand his crucial role in the lives of the Babylonian captives.

Ezekiel Was Deported to Babylon in 597 B.C.

Although Nebuchadnezzar's army leveled Jerusalem in 586 B.C., two deportations preceded that crushing blow—one in 605 and one in 597. Ezekiel was among the captives taken in 597, when Jehoiachin and his court surrendered to Nebuchadnezzar (see 2 Kings 24:8–17). According to the information provided in

EZEKIEL

About the Prophet	Judgment on Judah	Judgment on the Nations	Restoration of God's People
EZEKIEL'S CALL AND COMMISSION	GOD'S GLORY DEPARTS	ALL NATIONS ANSWER TO GOD	GOD'S GLORY RETURNS
God's hand on him			
God's word in him			
God's message through him			
CHAPTERS 1–3	*CHAPTERS 4–24*	*CHAPTERS 25–32*	*CHAPTERS 33–48*

Key Verse	39:28
Theme	God will be known through His judgment and restoration; God is sovereign over heaven and earth.
Christ in Ezekiel	The tender twig that becomes a stately cedar (17:22–24); the caring shepherd (ch. 34)

Ezekiel 1:1–3, he was twenty-five at the time of his exile (597 B.C.) and received his call to prophesy at age thirty (593 B.C.).[1]

Ezekiel came from a priestly family. Priests normally entered the service of the Lord at age thirty (see Num. 4:3). With no temple in which to serve, Ezekiel was called as a prophet to declare God's word and display His character among a people who had been ripped from their religious context.

The temple and its activities, though physically absent from among the exiles, are prominent in Ezekiel's words. Even the prophet's name, which means "God strengthens" or "strengthened by God,"[2] communicates the powerful presence of the Lord with His people.

Ezekiel's ministry differed from Daniel's, another exilic prophet, who was taken to Babylon in the first deportation (605 B.C.). While God placed Daniel in an administrative position in Babylon's royal court to reveal His plan for the ages to pagan kings, Ezekiel lived among the people of God, calling them to holiness and comforting them with hope. God indeed made His presence known during the exile—to conquerors and conquered alike.

Ezekiel's Whole Life Was a Message

Ezekiel communicated in pictures and words. His life was a stage upon which God acted out His drama of judgment and restoration—a human visual aid in God's exilic classroom.

For example, the prophet packed his belongings and dug through the wall of his house to picture Judah's exile (chap. 12). He told parables about vines (chap. 15) and allegories of birth (16:1–6) to picture God's care for His people. In a vision, he prophesied to dry bones and made them live, symbolizing new life for Judah and Israel (chap. 37).

Another intriguing way God used Ezekiel was to make him mute, except when he had a word from the Lord to declare (3:26–27). This divinely-controlled silence lasted seven years, ending only when Jerusalem's destruction confirmed his prophetic message.[3]

1. Most commentators agree that the "thirtieth year" (1:1) refers to Ezekiel's age, not the reign of a king. When his ministry began, the destruction of Jerusalem was still seven years away.

2. Bruce Wilkinson and Kenneth Boa, *Talk Thru the Old Testament*, vol. 1 of *Talk Thru the Bible* (Nashville, Tenn.: Thomas Nelson Publishers, 1983), p. 213.

3. Charles H. Dyer, "Ezekiel," in *The Bible Knowledge Commentary*, Old Testament edition, ed. John F. Walvoord and Roy B. Zuck (Wheaton, Ill.: Scripture Press Publications, Victor Books, 1985), pp. 1234, 1293.

Perhaps Ezekiel's most personally painful lesson, though, was the loss of his wife. When the Lord took from Ezekiel the "desire of [his] eyes" (24:16), He told the prophet not to mourn publicly for her. This was to instruct the exiles not to weep over the impending destruction of the temple in Jerusalem, the desire of their eyes, but "waste away because of [their] sins and groan among [them]selves" (v. 23 NIV).

Ezekiel's life reminds us that faithfully communicating God's Word can be personally costly.

God Had His Hand on Ezekiel

The strong hand of God was on His prophet, which seems obvious but is of crucial importance—especially for the exiles. They had no temple, no priestly structure, no sacrificial system through which God's glory could flow. God had to shine through people. So He chose such individuals as Ezekiel to herald His holiness, His heart, His hope.

When God wants to be known through an individual, He first puts His hand *on* that life. Then He speaks *to* that life. Only then does He speak *through* that life. An earthen vessel cannot refresh others with living water until it has first been fetched and filled by the Server.

We've met the man. Now let's take a closer look at the book he authored.

A Look at the Main Themes

Authors Wilkinson and Boa explain some of the book's characteristic themes:

> Ezekiel places a strong emphasis on the sovereignty, glory, and faithfulness of God. He concentrates on the temple with its perversion, destruction, and restoration. Another temple-related theme is Ezekiel's fascinating portrayal of God's heavenly glory (1:28; 3:12, 23), God's departing glory (9:3; 10:4, 18–19; 11:22–23), and God's earthly glory (43:1–5; 44:4). The sovereign purpose of God through judgment and blessing alike is that His people come to know that He is the Lord.[4]

4. Wilkinson and Boa, *Talk Thru the Old Testament*, p. 214.

More than sixty times in the book, God said He acted so that people would "know that I am the Lord." How ironic that God had to take such drastic measures to be known by His own people—those who should have known Him best. That says something about God's persistent love, doesn't it? If He did not love us, He would not bother to pursue us, He would not care if we remained distant from Him. But He does care. And He takes the initiative in keeping us close to His heart.

A Survey of the Content

Ezekiel, like Jeremiah, deals with God's judgment on Judah, His judgment of the nations, and His restoration of His people.

Chapters 1–3 show us God's commissioning of the prophet. The next major section (chaps. 4–24) portrays Judah's sins and pronounces Judah's judgments. The Gentile nations are judged next (chaps. 25–32). And finally, the return of God's glory and eternal presence with His people are foretold (chaps. 33–48).

Ezekiel's Call (Chaps. 1–3)

Ezekiel had settled by the Chebar river (1:1), which was actually a canal that connected to the Euphrates River in Babylon. There God appeared to him in a vision. And what a vision it was. Ezekiel saw four angelic beings in the midst of a flashing cloud of fire. Each of these creatures, as Stuart Briscoe describes,

> had four wings, two of which were stretched out to join with the wings of the next creature to form the base of a large platform on which was something resembling a throne (1:11, 26). Beside the creatures were massive wheels full of eyes! (1:18) The whole platform and throne moved with lightning speed, with a great whirring sound (1:14).[5]

Flashing lights. Strange beings. Whirring wheels. UFO enthusiasts have tried to use Ezekiel's vision as biblical evidence for life on other planets. But the prophet wasn't having that kind of close encounter. He was standing in the presence of "the likeness of the glory of the Lord" (1:28). And all he could do was fall on his face.

---

5. Stuart Briscoe, *Dry Bones* (Wheaton, Ill.: Scripture Press Publications, Victor Books, 1977), p. 12.

A survey is inadequate for presenting all the details of the vision and their various interpretations. The most important point to remember, as author Stuart Briscoe tells us, is that

> the One seated on the throne is the focal point of the vision. Everything else is designed to illustrate some aspect of His Being and action.[6]

So, like Isaiah and Jeremiah, Ezekiel "was prepared for his ministry by receiving a vision of the glory and majesty of God before he was called to serve the Lord."[7]

God commissioned Ezekiel to take His words to the "rebellious house" of Israel[8] (chap. 2)—a designation that applied primarily to the exiles but also to those who remained in Jerusalem. The Lord also empowered the prophet with His Spirit, "fed" him His Word, charged him with faithful delivery of it, then sent him to face a people with a deplorable response record (chap. 3).

Judgments against Judah (Chaps. 4–24)

Through object lessons, signs, sermons, and parables, Ezekiel communicated the causes, certainty, and severity of God's coming judgment on Judah. Even though the exiles wouldn't have been in Jerusalem when it fell, God still wanted them to know that they bore responsibility for its destruction.

Following God's instructions, Ezekiel sketched a likeness of Jerusalem on a clay tablet, then "besieged" it, showing the imminent fate of the holy city (chap. 4). He also shaved his head and beard and divided the hair for different purposes. One third he burned, another third he sliced with a sword, and a final third he scattered to the wind (5:2). This symbolized God's wrath against Jerusalem, who "has rebelled against My ordinances more wickedly than the nations and against My statutes more than the lands which surround her" (v. 6). However, Ezekiel also tucked away some strands of hair in his robe, depicting God's preservation of a remnant (v. 3).

God's judgment would also fall on the mountains of Judah,

---

6. Briscoe, *Dry Bones*, p. 12.

7. Dyer, "Ezekiel," p. 1227.

8. Ezekiel demonstrates that the name *Israel* can designate the people of God in general, not just the northern kingdom, sometimes called Samaria by the prophet, which had already fallen to Assyria. His use of *Israel* also looks forward to the reunification of Israel and Judah (see Ezek. 37:15–22).

where the high places, sites of pagan worship erected by the Jews, would crumble (chap. 6). Chapter 7 highlights the inevitability of Jerusalem's destruction.

In another vision, the prophet witnessed idolatry in God's temple, and he saw God slaughter those who practiced and supported it (chaps. 8–9). Since the temple had been desecrated for so long, God withdrew His glory from it (chap. 10).

The Lord next showed Ezekiel His judgment of apostate leaders. Yet in the midst of His wrathful revelation, God promised that a remnant would return to the land and worship Him (chap. 11).

> "And I shall give them one heart, and shall put a new spirit within them. And I shall take the heart of stone out of their flesh and give them a heart of flesh, that they may walk in My statutes and keep My ordinances, and do them. Then they will be My people, and I shall be their God." (11:19–20)

[handwritten margin note: God has hardened hearts; now He has given willingness]

Chapters 12–24 address

> the causes and extent of Judah's coming judgment through dramatic signs, powerful sermons, and parables. Judah's prophets are counterfeits and her elders are idolatrous. They have become a fruitless vine and an adulterous wife. Babylon will swoop down like an eagle and pluck them up, and they will not be aided by Egypt. The people are responsible for their own sins, and they are not being unjustly judged for the sins of their ancestors. Judah has been unfaithful, but God promises that her judgment ultimately will be followed by restoration.[9]

As Ezekiel says about the heart of God, He desires life for us and not death.

> "Do I have any pleasure in the death of the wicked," declares the Lord God, "rather than that he should turn from his ways and live? . . . For I have no pleasure in the death of anyone who dies," declares the Lord God. "Therefore, repent and live." (18:23, 32)

9. Wilkinson and Boa, *Talk Thru the Old Testament*, p. 216.

Judgment on the Gentiles (Chaps. 25–32)

Because Judah's neighbors gloated over her demise, God was quick to remind them that they were next in line for His judgment. Ammon, Moab, Edom, and Philistia (chap. 25) were Israel's closest neighbors and oldest enemies.

Three chapters (chaps. 26–28) are devoted to Tyre, a wealthy trade city on the shore of the Mediterranean, which Nebuchadnezzar besieged for thirteen years. Alexander conquered the city 240 years later.[10] Sidon, just twenty miles north of Tyre, also fell to Nebuchadnezzar. God told Ezekiel,

> "No longer will the people of Israel have malicious neighbors who are painful briers and sharp thorns. Then they will know that I am the Sovereign Lord." (28:24 NIV)

Chapters 29–32 contain a series of oracles against Egypt, which foretell that

> unlike the nations in chapters 25–28 that were destroyed by Nebuchadnezzar, Egypt will continue to exist, but as "the lowliest of the kingdoms." Since that time it has never recovered its former glory or influence.[11]

Restoration of God's People (Chaps. 33–48)

As God's appointed watchman, Ezekiel carried the weight of Israel's souls on his shoulders. He had the responsibility of confronting God's people with their sins and warning them of coming judgment (chap. 33). When Nebuchadnezzar destroyed Jerusalem, God's judgments became a reality. So the Lord shifted His attention to comforting His people with the promise of restoration.

After Ezekiel heard the news of Jerusalem's fall, his first message of comfort was that the Lord would be Israel's Great Shepherd. Since the shepherds God had appointed had ignored and abused the sheep for personal gain (34:1–10), He promised to care for His flock personally.

---

10. Merrill F. Unger, *The New Unger's Bible Dictionary*, revised and updated edition, ed. R. K. Harrison, Howard F. Vos, and Cyril J. Barber (Chicago, Ill.: Moody Press, 1988), see "Tyre."

11. Wilkinson and Boa, *Talk Thru the Old Testament*, p. 216.

For thus says the Lord God, "Behold, I Myself will search for My sheep and seek them out. As a shepherd cares for his herd in the day when he is among his scattered sheep, so I will care for My sheep and will deliver them from all the places to which they were scattered on a cloudy and gloomy day. And I will bring them out from the peoples and gather them from the countries and bring them to their own land; and I will feed them on the mountains of Israel, by the streams, and in all the inhabited places of the land. I will feed them in a good pasture, and their grazing ground will be on the mountain heights of Israel. There they will lie down in good grazing ground, and they will feed in rich pasture on the mountains of Israel. I will feed My flock and I will lead them to rest," declares the Lord God. "I will seek the lost, bring back the scattered, bind up the broken, and strengthen the sick; but the fat and the strong I will destroy. I will feed them with judgment." (34:11–16)

What a reminder that, though our earthly spiritual leaders are imperfect, Jesus Christ, the Good Shepherd, cares for us with infallible love and perfect provision.

The Lord promised that His people would rise from the ruins of judgment to new life. "I will give you a new heart and put a new spirit within you," He reiterated. "And I will remove the heart of stone from your flesh and give you a heart of flesh" (36:26; see also 11:19; 18:31).

Like the dry bones in Ezekiel's vision that miraculously regenerated into living beings, the exiled Jews would be revitalized, cleansed and reunited into one nation—under one messianic King (chap. 37).

In chapters 40–48, God rounded out the picture of restoration with a detailed description of a new temple—complete with priestly duties and sacrifices—as well as a new city and new land for God's people.

The design of this temple varies from those of the temples built under Solomon (during the unified kingdom), Zerubbabel (after the exile), and Herod (around the time of Christ). Therefore, this section of Ezekiel poses some interpretational challenges.

Archaeological and biblical evidence confirms that Ezekiel's temple has never actually been built. Some scholars, therefore, believe it will be built during the Millennium, the one-thousand-year reign of Christ on earth, when God will fulfill all His promises to Israel.

Others interpret this section more figuratively, seeing it as a representation of the church's ministry in the present age. Proponents of this view argue that reinstating the sacrificial system—when Jesus Christ, the ultimate sacrifice, is present on earth—would be spiritual regression instead of progression.

Eerdmans Handbook to the Bible captures the essence of the temple's importance:

> Although, for the most part, [chapters 40–48] make rather dull reading, they are in a very real sense, the climax to the whole book. Ezekiel began with a vision of God in the plains of Babylon. It ends with a vision of God returning in glory to a new temple— God in the midst of his people once again, never to depart.[12]

God's judgment is severe. But there is comfort in knowing that an eternity of His glorious presence awaits those He has chosen for Himself.

> "And the name of the city from that time on will be:
>
> THE LORD IS THERE."
>
> (48:35b NIV)

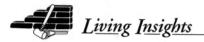 *Living Insights*

Behind our personal pain, there is a providential God who wants to be known—by us and by the people who observe us.

That's one of the practical lessons Ezekiel teaches. The prophet endured all kinds of inconvenience (leaning on his side for 430

---

12. David and Pat Alexander, eds., *Eerdmans Handbook to the Bible* (1973; reprint, Grand Rapids, Mich.: William B. Eerdmans Publishing Co., 1983), p. 429.

days) and anguish (the death of his wife) to model God's truth. The prophet's perspective must have been much larger than the confines of his present life for him to go through such turmoil and still walk with God, still see Him as good, still comply with His wishes.

Though God doesn't call us to act out direct prophecies today, we still communicate something about Him by the way we live. And that includes the times when living is especially hard.

When a Christian family member dies, for example, we can grieve with hope, thus offering comfort to others.

In the aftermath of an untimely job loss, we can extend grace and forgiveness toward our former employer and, while we actively seek new employment, trust God for our provision.

In the midst of mundane duties, we can emanate a higher purpose, commitment, and joy.

You're right. None of these are easy. But, like Ezekiel, we have God's Word and Spirit to guide us in the way of Christlikeness.

> "Let your light shine before men in such a way that they may see your good works, and glorify your Father who is in heaven." (Matt. 5:16)

Chapter 14

DANIEL: MAN OF INTEGRITY, MESSAGE OF PROPHECY

A Survey of Daniel

O f all the Bible's heroes, Daniel is perhaps the most difficult to fit into a category. Though he saw visions of the future, he wasn't the same kind of prophet as Amos or Isaiah.[1] Though he interceded for his people, he wasn't a priest. Though he was a confidant of kings, he wasn't royalty. And though he witnessed mighty battles, he wasn't a warrior.

In many ways, Daniel was an ordinary Jew, like thousands of other exiles from Judah forced to live in Babylon. Yet God's hand was on Daniel's life in an extraordinary way. By bringing him before kings and preserving him through the entire seventy-year captivity, the Lord used him to model godliness for His people . . . and for us.

The book of Daniel is more than stories about fiery furnaces, lions' dens, and fantastic visions. It's about seeing God for who He is, the sovereign ruler of the nations, and living for Him with integrity and faith.

Background

Though Daniel bent his knee to human kings, he bent his life to the King of Kings—the God of Israel, whose kingdom will never end. Daniel lived in light of what his name meant, "God is my judge."[2]

Historical Backdrop

Daniel was among those exiled in Nebuchadnezzar's first assault on Jerusalem in 605 B.C., nineteen years before the city was finally sacked in 586. Babylon's fury shook the Jews' faith. They had always believed that a descendent of David would occupy the throne until the coming of the Messiah and His reign of peace, and that the temple would stand for all time as an inviolable channel between heaven and earth.

---

1. The Hebrew Bible doesn't list his book with the Prophets but places it with the Writings, following the book of Esther.

2. Bruce Wilkinson and Kenneth Boa, *Talk Thru the Old Testament*, vol. 1 of *Talk Thru the Bible* (Nashville, Tenn.: Thomas Nelson Publishers, 1983), p. 221.

DANIEL

Biographical Section
Daniel Interprets Others' Dreams

MAIN EMPHASIS:
DANIEL THE PROPHET

Introduction and setting *(1)*

Nebuchadnezzar's apocalyptic dream *(2)*

Historical narratives (political and personal) *(3–6)*

*CHAPTERS
1–6*

Prophetical Section
Angel Interprets Daniel's Dreams

MAIN EMPHASIS:
THE PROPHECIES OF DANIEL

Daniel's foundational vision *(7)*

Prophetic visions (near and far) *(8–12)*

*CHAPTERS
7–12*

POLITICAL POWERS	. . . IN DANIEL'S DAY		. . . AND AFTERWARD
Babylonian Rule Nebuchadnezzar Belshazzar	**Medo-Persian Rule** Darius Cyrus	**Grecian Rule** Alexander the Great Four Generals	**Roman Rule** Last of the Gentile powers

Key Verses	2:20–22, 44; 4:34–37
Theme	God's sovereignty over kingdoms and His unfolding plan for the future
Christ in Daniel	The stone that will crush earth's kingdoms (2:34–35, 44); Son of Man (7:13–14); the coming Messiah who will be crucified (9:25–26)

Yet, in less than twenty years, everything on which the Jews had built their faith was gone, ground into dust by the Babylonians. To make matters worse, the Lord Himself was behind the downfall, handing the king of Judah to Nebuchadnezzar, along with sacred articles of the temple (Dan. 1:1–2).

Issues at Hand

The people knew that God was disciplining them for their disobedience, but how far would He go? Would He abandon His promises altogether? Did He still care for His people? Commentator Ronald Wallace gets to the core questions troubling the Jews' hearts:

> Could God really use a pagan like Nebuchadnezzar in any way as an instrument for their good or for their education? Were they really expected to believe that when they were in his brutal hands they were still in the hands of God?[3]

Daniel's book answers these questions with resounding assurance that God had not forgotten them. He would walk beside them through their valley of discipline, moving people and events according to His divine purposes. Also, though the Jews lived as a minority in a foreign culture, Daniel showed them they could still trust the Lord and serve Him with integrity and faith in a world of compromise and fear. And so can we.

A Word about Apocalyptic Literature

The prophecies in Daniel differ in style and content from those of the other writing prophets. All of the other prophets prefaced their messages or visions with phrases such as, "Thus says the Lord" or "The word of the Lord." Their words and actions conveyed the divine message, which usually addressed the people's sins, warned of God's judgment, urged repentance, and comforted with restoration.

In Daniel, however, visions and dreams of a highly symbolic nature communicate the message of the future. Daniel does not guide his people toward God with direct rebukes or encouragement. He doesn't address the issues of social justice or true worship. Rather, his prophecies are *apocalyptic*, a literary form marked by these themes:

that God is in control of history, that pagan empires

---

3. Ronald S. Wallace, *The Message of Daniel: The Lord Is King*, The Bible Speaks Today Series (Downers Grove, Ill.: InterVarsity Press, n.d.), pp. 30–31.

survive only for as long as he permits, and that the "end" will come at a time he has appointed. This final great event amounts to a new creation in which there will be no evil or suffering; even death itself will be conquered. The kingdom of God will replace all earthly empires forever; the nations may share in this salvation but the oppressors of Israel, and the unfaithful within Israel, will be judged.[4]

Rather than focusing on human responsibility, apocalyptic prophecy focuses on God's sovereign intervention. Its purpose is to encourage God's people with the glorious future He has planned for them. And this is just what Daniel does.

Structure of the Book

The first six chapters of Daniel's book focus mostly on events in his life. Each vignette highlights a showdown between the kingdom of earth and the kingdom of heaven. The last six chapters contain Daniel's prophetic visions of the future.

Interestingly, Daniel wrote the first chapter of his book in Hebrew but switched to Aramaic, the language of the Gentiles, in chapters 2 through 7, as if to target the Gentiles with his message. In chapters 8 through 12, he wrote in Hebrew again to highlight the future of the Jews under Gentile domination.

Biographical Section (Daniel 1–6)

Daniel's life exudes integrity. From beginning to end, through each crisis of faith, Daniel stayed unwaveringly true to his Lord.

Taking a Stand as a Teenager (Chap. 1)

Wishing to assimilate promising young Jews into his service, King Nebuchadnezzar gave Daniel a new Babylonian name and immersed him in Chaldean philosophy and language. He even tried to change his diet, giving him choice food that, in all likelihood, had been offered to idols. Daniel, however, determined not to defile himself with the king's food. Instead, he tactfully proposed a ten-day test in which he and his friends would eat only vegetables. Since Daniel honored God, God honored him by granting his plan success

4. *New Concise Bible Dictionary*, ed. Derek Williams (Downers Grove, Ill.: InterVarsity Press, 1989), see "apocalyptic."

and by giving him great wisdom and the ability to interpret dreams.

The king gave the orders, but it was clear from the start that God set the course for Daniel's life.

Nebuchadnezzar's Apocalyptic Dream (Chap. 2)

God sets the course for the whole world too, as Nebuchadnezzar soon found out. In a dream, the king saw a giant statue crushed by a stone. None of Babylon's wise men could tell him the dream, let alone interpret it. God, however, answered Daniel's prayers and showed him the dream and the interpretation. The metals in the statue represented history's great world powers—the gold head was Babylon; the silver chest and arms, Medo-Persia; the bronze belly and thighs, Greece; and the legs of iron, Rome. The feet of iron and clay symbolize an unstable extension of the Roman Empire, perhaps an alliance of western powers in the future. The stone is the Messiah, who will destroy the kingdoms of the world at the end of time to set up His own kingdom—the mountain that fills the earth.[5]

On seeing God's design for the future, Daniel exclaimed the theme of the book:

> "Let the name of God be blessed forever and ever,
> For wisdom and power belong to Him.
> And it is He who changes the times and the epochs;
> He removes kings and establishes kings;
> He gives wisdom to wise men,
> And knowledge to men of understanding."
> (2:20–21)

The Golden Image and Fiery Furnace (Chap. 3)

In chapter 3, Daniel's friends Shadrach, Meshach, and Abednego refused to bow down to Nebuchadnezzar's golden colossus and were thrown into a fiery furnace. However, neither the king's raging anger nor the raging flames could touch them. When they emerged from the fire unsinged, the king acknowledged their God and decreed that anyone who spoke against Him would be punished.

---

5. This vision covers the period called "the times of the Gentiles" (Luke 21:24). It lasts from Nebuchadnezzar's invasion of Judah to the second coming of the Messiah. During this period, Gentile powers dominate the nation of Israel and no descendant of David sits on the throne. The times of the Gentiles will end when Christ returns at the end of the Tribulation to fulfill the covenantal promises to Israel and establish the millennial kingdom.

The Humbling of a King (Chap. 4)

In chapter 4, the king had a dream about a tree cut down to a stump. Again, only Daniel was empowered to interpret its meaning, which was a message to Nebuchadnezzar: if he wouldn't humble himself before God, he would be cut down. Later, the prideful king boasted of his own glory, so God reduced him to the level of a beast for seven years. When he recovered from his insanity, he worshiped God in what many think was a genuine personal conversion.

The Handwriting on Babylon's Wall (Chap. 5)

Nebuchadnezzar's grandson, Belshazzar, did not learn from his grandfather's experience. He profaned the articles of God's temple by using them to toast his gods, so God interrupted his raucous party with a divine message written on the palace wall. Daniel was called in to decipher its meaning—it spelled out Belshazzar's death and the doom of the Babylonian empire.

Darius and the Lions' Den (Chap. 6)

By now in his eighties, the venerable Daniel so impressed the new leader, Darius, that he wanted to put him in charge of running the kingdom. The other officials wanted the power for themselves, however, so they devised a way to entrap Daniel. Making it illegal to pray to anyone besides the king, they arrested Daniel as he worshiped the Lord. King Darius had no choice but to throw his faithful friend to the lions. God, however, shut the mouths of the beasts, along with the mouths of Daniel's critics. Once again, a new kingdom met and bowed to the eternal king.

Prophetic Section (Daniel 7–12)

Having established his integrity and credibility in the first six chapters, Daniel then revealed his fantastic and often frightening apocalyptic prophecies.

Daniel's Foundational Vision (Chap. 7)

In chapter 7, Daniel recorded his dream about four nightmarish animals. Each beast parallels the four metals in Nebuchadnezzar's dream of the statue (chap. 2): the winged lion represents Babylon; the bear with one side raised, Medo-Persia; the four-headed leopard, Greece; and the terrible beast with ten horns, Rome. In a broader sense, the beast also represents future western powers from which ten nations will join forces in a coalition of power. Another horn will arise as their leader, who will rule for "a time, times, and half a time"—that is, three and a half years (v. 25). This is the Antichrist, who will rule the earth during the last half of the Tribulation (see Rev. 13). However, as Daniel saw, his rule will be broken by the Son of Man, Jesus Christ, who will receive dominion from God and then hand it to His followers (Dan. 7:27).

The Vision of the Ram and the Goat (Chap. 8)

The ram and goat in chapter 8 reveal the Jews under the Medo-Persian and Greek empires, respectively. The one-horned goat slams into the ram, trampling it in victory. So Greece conquered Persia. Later, the goat's large horn breaks but sprouts four horns in its place, symbolizing the sudden death of Alexander the Great and the rise of the four generals who succeeded him. Out of one horn grows a smaller horn, who magnifies himself, removes the regular sacrifice in the temple, and persecutes the Jews. This is Antiochus IV Epiphanes—a type of the Antichrist to come, who will "oppose the Prince of princes [Jesus Christ]" but be "broken without human agency" (v. 25).

A Prayer and an Answer (Chap. 9)

Realizing that the seventy-year period that Jeremiah had predicted for Judah's captivity was almost over (see Jer. 25:11–12), Daniel prayed that God would restore His people (Dan. 9:1–19). In response, God agreed to allow His people to return to their homeland, but He also sent Gabriel to unveil a greater revelation to Daniel—a period of "seventy weeks," or seventy units of seven years each. Through this prophecy, God revealed several future events: Jesus' triumphal entry into Jerusalem, the Crucifixion, the seven-year tribulation period, the covenant between the Antichrist and the Jews, the desecration of the temple, and the second coming of Christ.

An Angelic Vision (Chap. 10)

Chapter 10 records Daniel's vision of an angel who brought him a terrifying message. Just as startling as the forthcoming message was the picture of spiritual warfare among angelic beings. On the way to give Daniel God's message, the angel was accosted by "the prince of the kingdom of Persia" and delayed twenty-one days. Only with the help of a stronger angel, Michael, did he prevail and get to Daniel (v. 13).

The Angel's Message (Chap. 11)

Chapter 11 reveals the angel's message, which contains amazingly detailed predictions of the wars between Medo-Persia and Greece and between the dynasties of the Ptolemies (Egypt) and the Seleucids (Syria). The wicked Antiochus IV Epiphanes appears again as a type of the Antichrist to come, who will destroy many but "will come to his end, and no one will help him" (v. 45).

The End of Time (Chap. 12)

The angel's prophecy concludes with a beacon of hope. Michael, the angel of the Jews, will rescue God's people during the Antichrist's reign of terror, and those who have remained faithful to God will be ushered into everlasting life. For the wise and steadfast Daniel, the angel had a special promise: "You will enter into rest and rise again for your allotted portion at the end of the age" (v. 13).

Lessons from Daniel

From Daniel's life and writings we learn that *a person of integrity is a powerful instrument in the hand of God*. A life of integrity may lead us into a lions' den of misunderstanding and ridicule. But there's nothing like the freedom and power that God gives those who are determined to do what is right, no matter what the cost.

Also, we learn that *a promise with authority is a calm assurance*. The prophecies in Daniel weren't meant to frighten but comfort us. The world may be breaking apart around us, but God is still in control. He is King, regardless of who sits on the thrones of earth. And those who follow Him will triumph in the end.

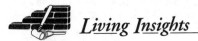 *Living Insights*

The vision of God's glorious, triumphant future gives us hope.[6] Hope has been defined as "a willing, trusting anticipation of what God will do."[7] Not a weak, "oh, I wish God would do that" sentiment.

---

6. This Living Insight has been adapted from the study guide *Daniel: God's Pattern for the Future*, coauthored by Bryce Klabunde, from the Bible-teaching ministry of Charles R. Swindoll (Anaheim, Calif.: Insight for Living, 1996), pp. 8–9.

7. A. J. Conyers, *The End: What Jesus Really Said about the Last Things* (Downers Grove, Ill.: InterVarsity Press, 1995), pp. 50–51.

But a *trusting anticipation*, a confident expectation of what He *will* do.

What will Christ do when He bursts through history at the end of the age? For starters, He'll restore justice—no more criminals getting off the hook, no more victims denied their dignity and their cause. He'll put an end to evil and suffering. He'll create the perfect world—peaceful, happy, holy. Best of all, He'll give us His presence. After such a long wait, God's children will finally get to see their Savior.

That's something to anticipate, isn't it! What else did the angel tell Daniel he could anticipate (see Dan. 12:2–3)?

_____

_____

_____

What qualities would bring God's luminous rewards (v. 3)?

_____

_____

Do we have to wait for Christ's second coming to have these mark our characters today? Of course not. The hope of a glorious future energizes us to pursue righteousness and insight, as well as Daniel's legacy of integrity and faith, *now.*

We could summarize prophecy's impact this way: prophetic vision gives us hope, hope fills us with confident anticipation, and anticipation energizes us to live for God today. God doesn't give us knowledge about the future so we can stand around craning our necks toward heaven, speculating on the time of His arrival. He gives us prophecy to drive us forward. To encourage us. To change us.

Are you ready for change?

BOOKS FOR PROBING FURTHER

What a concert! One more volume and you will have made it through the entire Old Testament. While we tune up for volume 3, covering Hosea through Malachi, pour yourself a cool drink and peruse the following suggested reading list. During this intermission, you'll have a little time to run out and purchase one or two books to deepen your study of Ezra through Daniel. See you right back here for the rest of the concert!

Alexander, David and Pat, eds. *Eerdmans Handbook to the Bible*. 1973. Reprint, Grand Rapids, Mich.: William B. Eerdmans Publishing Co., 1983.

Bright, John. *A History of Israel*. 3d ed. Philadelphia, Pa.: Westminster Press, 1981.

Clowney, Edmund P. *The Unfolding Mystery: Discovering Christ in the Old Testament*. Colorado Springs, Colo.: NavPress, 1988.

Glickman, S. Craig. *A Song for Lovers*. Downers Grove, Ill.: InterVarsity Press, 1976.

Kidner, Derek. *The Message of Jeremiah: Against Wind and Tide*. The Bible Speaks Today series. Downers Grove, Ill.: InterVarsity Press, 1987.

Lee-Thorp, Karen. *The Story of Stories*. Rev. ed. Colorado Springs, Colo.: NavPress, 1995.

Mason, Mike. *The Gospel According to Job*. Wheaton, Ill.: Good News Publishers, Crossway Books, 1994.

Peterson, Eugene H. *Five Smooth Stones for Pastoral Work*. Atlanta, Ga.: John Knox Press, 1980.

———. The Message: *The Wisdom Books*. Colorado Springs, Colo.: NavPress, 1996.

Swindoll, Charles R. *Hand Me Another Brick*. Nashville, Tenn.: Thomas Nelson Publishers, 1978.

Walvoord, John F., and Roy B. Zuck, eds. *The Bible Knowledge Commentary*. Old Testament edition. Wheaton, Ill.: Scripture Press Publications, Victor Books, 1985.

Wilkinson, Bruce, and Kenneth Boa. *Talk Thru the Bible*. Nashville, Tenn.: Thomas Nelson Publishers, 1983.

Some of these books may be out of print and available only through a library. For those currently available, please contact your local Christian bookstore. Books by Charles R. Swindoll may be obtained through Insight for Living. IFL also offers some books by other authors—please note the ordering information that follows and contact the office that serves you.

ORDERING INFORMATION

GOD'S MASTERWORK
Volume Two
Cassette Tapes and Study Guide

This Bible study guide was designed to be used independently or in conjunction with the broadcast of Chuck Swindoll's taped messages which are listed below. If you would like to order cassette tapes or further copies of this study guide, please see the information given below and the order form provided at the end of this guide.

		U.S.	Canada
GM2	Study guide	$ 4.95	$ 6.50
GM2CS	Cassette series, includes all individual tapes, album cover, and one complimentary study guide	46.75	53.75
GM2 1–7	Individual cassettes, includes messages A and B	6.00	7.48

Prices are subject to change without notice.

GM2 1-A: *Ezra: True Man of the Word*—A Survey of Ezra
   B: *Nehemiah: Softhearted Hard Hat*—A Survey of Nehemiah

GM2 2-A: *Esther: The Beauty and the Best*—A Survey of Esther
   B: *Job: Magnificent Man of Misery*—A Survey of Job

GM2 3-A: *Psalms: Inspired Anthology of Praise*—A Survey of Psalms
   B: *Proverbs: Reliable Counsel for Right Living*— A Survey of Proverbs

GM2 4-A: *Ecclesiastes: Searching for the Meaning of Life*— A Survey of Ecclesiastes
   B: *Song of Solomon: Poem of Faithful Love*— A Survey of Song of Solomon

GM2 5-A: *Profile of a Prophet*—Selected Scriptures
   B: *Isaiah: Prince among the Prophets*—A Survey of Isaiah

GM2 6-A: *Jeremiah: Weeping, Warning, and Waiting*— A Survey of Jeremiah
   B: *Lamentations: A Prophet's Broken Heart*— A Survey of Lamentations

GM2 7-A: *Ezekiel: Strong Man of God*—A Survey of Ezekiel
  B: *Daniel: Man of Integrity, Message of Prophecy*—
  A Survey of Daniel

HOW TO ORDER BY PHONE OR FAX
(Credit card orders only)

Web site: http://www.insight.org

United States: 1-800-772-8888 or FAX (714) 575-5684, 24 hours a day, 7 days a week

Canada: 1-800-663-7639 or FAX (604) 532-7173, 24 hours a day, 7 days a week

Australia and the South Pacific: (03) 9877-4277 from 8:00 A.M. to 5:00 P.M., Monday through Friday.
FAX (03) 9877-4077 anytime, day or night

Other International Locations: call the International Ordering Services Department in the United States at (714) 575-5000 from 8:00 A.M. to 4:30 P.M., Pacific time, Monday through Friday
FAX (714) 575-5683 anytime, day or night

HOW TO ORDER BY MAIL

United States
• Mail to: Mail Center
      Insight for Living
      Post Office Box 69000
      Anaheim, CA 92817-0900
• Sales tax: California residents add 7.75%.
• Shipping and handling charges must be added to each order. See chart on order form for amount.
• Payment: personal checks, money orders, credit cards (Visa, MasterCard, Discover Card, and American Express). No invoices or COD orders available.
• $10 fee for *any* returned check.

Canada
• Mail to: Insight for Living Ministries
      Post Office Box 2510
      Vancouver, BC V6B 3W7
• Sales tax: please add 7% GST. British Columbia residents also add 7% sales tax (on tapes or cassette series).
• Shipping and handling charges must be added to each order. See chart on order form for amount.

- Payment: personal cheques, money orders, credit cards (Visa, Master-Card). No invoices or COD orders available.
- Delivery: approximately four weeks.

Australia and the South Pacific
- Mail to: Insight for Living, Inc.
  GPO Box 2823 EE
  Melbourne, Victoria 3001, Australia
- Shipping: add 25% to the total order.
- Delivery: approximately four to six weeks.
- Payment: personal checks payable in Australian funds, international money orders, or credit cards (Visa, MasterCard, and Bankcard).

United Kingdom and Europe
- Mail to: Insight for Living
  c/o Trans World Radio
  Post Office Box 1020
  Bristol BS99 1XS
  England, United Kingdom
- Shipping: add 25% to the total order.
- Delivery: approximately four to six weeks.
- Payment: cheques payable in sterling pounds or credit cards (Visa, MasterCard, and American Express).

Other International Locations
- Mail to: International Processing Services Department
  Insight for Living
  Post Office Box 69000
  Anaheim, CA 92817-0900
- Shipping and delivery time: please see chart that follows.
- Payment: personal checks payable in U.S. funds, international money orders, or credit cards (Visa, MasterCard, and American Express).

Type of Shipping	Postage Cost	Delivery
Surface	10% of total order*	6 to 10 weeks
Airmail	25% of total order*	under 6 weeks

*Use U.S. price as a base.

Our Guarantee: Your complete satisfaction is our top priority here at Insight for Living. If you're not completely satisfied with anything you order, please return it for full credit, a refund, or a replacement, as you prefer.

Insight for Living Catalog: The Insight for Living catalog features study guides, tapes, and books by a variety of Christian authors. To obtain a free copy, call us at the numbers listed above.

Order Form
United States, Australia, and Other International Locations
(Canadian residents please use order form on reverse side.)

GM2CS represents the entire *God's Masterwork, Volume Two* series in a special album cover, while GM2 1–7 are the individual tapes included in the series. GM2 represents this study guide, should you desire to order additional copies.

Product Code	Product Description	Qty	Price	Total
GM2	Study Guide		$ 4.95	$
GM2CS	Cassette Series with study guide		46.75	
GM2-	Individual cassette		6.00	
GM2-	Individual cassette		6.00	
GM2-	Individual cassette		6.00	

Subtotal

California Residents—Sales Tax
Add 7.75% of subtotal.

Amount of Order	First Class	UPS
$ 7.50 and under	1.00	4.00
$ 7.51 to 12.50	1.50	4.25
$12.51 to 25.00	3.50	4.50
$25.01 to 35.00	4.50	4.75
$35.01 to 60.00	5.50	5.25
$60.00 to 99.99	6.50	5.75
$100.00 and over	No Charge	

UPS ❑   First Class ❑
*Shipping must be added.
See chart for charges.*

Non-United States Residents
*Australia and Europe: add 25%.
Other: Price +10% surface or 25% airmail.*
Gift to Insight for Living
Tax-deductible in the United States.

Rush shipping and Fourth Class are also available. Please call for details.

Total Amount Due $
Please do not send cash.

Prices are subject to change without notice.

Payment by: ❑ Check or money order payable to Insight for Living or
❑ Visa ❑ MasterCard ❑ Discover Card ❑ American Express ❑ Bankcard (In Australia)

Number

Expiration Date ___ / ___   Signature

We cannot process your credit card purchase without your signature

Name:

Address:

City: State:

Zip Code: Country:

Telephone: (   )   –   Radio Station:

If questions arise concerning your order, we may need to contact you.

Mail this order form to the Mail Center at one of these addresses:

Insight for Living
Post Office Box 69000, Anaheim, CA 92817-0900

Insight for Living, Inc.
GPO Box 2823 EE, Melbourne, VIC 3001, Australia

ECFA
MEMBER

Order Form
Canadian Residents

(Residents of the United States, Australia, and other international locations, please use order form on reverse side.)

GM2CS represents the entire *God's Masterwork, Volume Two* series in a special album cover, while GM2 1–7 are the individual tapes included in the series. GM2 represents this study guide, should you desire to order additional copies.

Product Code	Product Description	Qty	Price	Total
GM2	Study Guide		$ 6.50	$
GM2CS	Cassette Series with study guide		53.75	
GM2-	Individual cassette		7.48	
GM2-	Individual cassette		7.48	
GM2-	Individual cassette		7.48	

Amount of Order	Canada Post
Orders to $10.00	2.00
$10.01 to 30.00	3.50
$30.01 to 50.00	5.00
$50.01 to 99.99	7.00
$100 and over	No charge

Loomis Courier is also available.
Please call for details.

Subtotal

Add 7% GST
British Columbia Residents
Add 7% sales tax on individual tapes or cassette series.

Shipping
Shipping must be added. See chart for charges.

Gift to Insight for Living Ministries
Tax-deductible in Canada.

Total Amount Due $
Please do not send cash.

Prices are subject to change without notice.

Payment by: ❑ Cheque or money order payable to Insight for Living Ministries or
❑ Visa ❑ MasterCard

Number

Expiration Date / Signature

We cannot process your credit card purchase without your signature.

Name:

Address:

City: Province:

Postal Code: Country:

Telephone: ( ) – Radio Station:

If questions arise concerning your order, we may need to contact you.

Mail this order form to the Processing Services Department at the following address:

Insight for Living Ministries
Post Office Box 2510
Vancouver, BC, Canada V6B 3W7

Order Form
United States, Australia, and Other International Locations
(Canadian residents please use order form on reverse side.)

GM2CS represents the entire *God's Masterwork, Volume Two* series in a special album cover, while GM2 1–7 are the individual tapes included in the series. GM2 represents this study guide, should you desire to order additional copies.

Product Code	Product Description	Qty	Price	Total
GM2	Study Guide		$ 4.95	$
GM2CS	Cassette Series with study guide		46.75	
GM2-	Individual cassette		6.00	
GM2-	Individual cassette		6.00	
GM2-	Individual cassette		6.00	

Subtotal

California Residents—Sales Tax
Add 7.75% of subtotal.

Amount of Order	First Class	UPS
$ 7.50 and under	1.00	4.00
$ 7.51 to 12.50	1.50	4.25
$12.51 to 25.00	3.50	4.50
$25.01 to 35.00	4.50	4.75
$35.01 to 60.00	5.50	5.25
$60.00 to 99.99	6.50	5.75
$100.00 and over	No Charge	

Rush shipping and Fourth Class are also available. Please call for details.

UPS ❑   First Class ❑
Shipping must be added.
See chart for charges.

Non-United States Residents
Australia and Europe: add 25%.
Other: Price +10% surface or 25% airmail.
Gift to Insight for Living
Tax-deductible in the United States.

Total Amount Due $
Please do not send cash.

Prices are subject to change without notice.

Payment by: ❑ Check or money order payable to Insight for Living or
❑ Visa   ❑ MasterCard   ❑ Discover Card   ❑ American Express   ❑ Bankcard (In Australia)

Number

Expiration Date /   Signature

We cannot process your credit card purchase without your signature

Name:

Address:

City: State:

Zip Code: Country:

Telephone: (   ) —   Radio Station:

If questions arise concerning your order, we may need to contact you.

Mail this order form to the Mail Center at one of these addresses:

Insight for Living
Post Office Box 69000, Anaheim, CA 92817-0900

Insight for Living, Inc.
GPO Box 2823 EE, Melbourne, VIC 3001, Australia

ECFA MEMBER

Order Form
Canadian Residents

(Residents of the United States, Australia, and other international locations,
please use order form on reverse side.)

GM2CS represents the entire *God's Masterwork, Volume Two* series in a special album cover,
while GM2 1–7 are the individual tapes included in the series. GM2 represents this study guide,
should you desire to order additional copies.

Product Code	Product Description	Qty	Price	Total
GM2	Study Guide		$ 6.50	$.
GM2CS	Cassette Series with study guide		53.75	.
GM2-	Individual cassette		7.48	.
GM2-	Individual cassette		7.48	.
GM2-	Individual cassette		7.48	.

		Subtotal	.
		Add 7% GST	.
		British Columbia Residents *Add 7% sales tax on individual tapes or cassette series.*	.
		Shipping *Shipping must be added. See chart for charges.*	.
		Gift to Insight for Living Ministries *Tax-deductible in Canada.*	.
		Total Amount Due $ *Please do not send cash.*	.

Amount of Order	Canada Post
Orders to $10.00	2.00
$10.01 to 30.00	3.50
$30.01 to 50.00	5.00
$50.01 to 99.99	7.00
$100 and over	No charge

Loomis Courier is also available.
Please call for details.

Prices are subject to change without notice.

Payment by: ❑ Cheque or money order payable to Insight for Living Ministries or
❑ Visa ❑ MasterCard

Number

Expiration Date / Signature

We cannot process your credit card purchase without your signature.

Name:

Address:

City: Province:

Postal Code: Country:

Telephone: ( ) – Radio Station:

If questions arise concerning your order, we may need to contact you.

Mail this order form to the Processing Services Department at the following address:

Insight for Living Ministries
Post Office Box 2510
Vancouver, BC, Canada V6B 3W7